Thinking about criminology

Thinking about criminology

Edited by

Simon Holdaway
Sheffield University
and
Paul Rock
London School of Economics

University of Toronto Press
Toronto Buffalo

First published in 1998 by UCL Press

First published in North America in 1998
by University of Toronto Press Incorporated
Toronto Buffalo

ISBNs 0-8020-4401-8 (cloth)
      0-8020-8208-4 (paper)

Canadian Cataloguing in Publication Data

Main entry under title:

Thinking about criminology

ISBN 0-8020-4401-8 (bound)   ISBN 0-8020-8208-4 (pbk.)

1. Criminology.   2. Deviant behavior.   I. Holdaway, Simon.
II. Rock, Paul Elliott.

HV6025.S64 1998   364   C98-930250-4

Typeset in Palatino by GCS, Leighton Buzzard, UK.
Printed by T.J. International, Padstow, UK.

Contents

Notes on contributors

Nils Christie is professor of criminology, Faculty of Law, University of Oslo, Norway. He is the author of numerous articles and 12 books about criminological subjects, several of them in English. *Limits to pain* (1981), is by now published in 12 languages. His most recent book is *Crime control as industry: towards GULAGS, western style?* (1993) will this year be published in seven languages. Most of his writing has been in the field of crime and crime control, but he has also published books on education, drugs, and on alternative communities – villages for extraordinary people, by many so-called mentally retarded.

Nils Christie has been a member of Royal Commissions in Norway on the organization of the police, dangerous criminals and educational matters. He has been the president of the Scandinavian Council for Criminology, and was for many years director of the Institute for Criminology and Penal Law in Norway. He is a member of Academy of Science in Norway (Oslo) and in Sweden (Lund). He has been invited as a visiting professor several terms to Berkeley, California, Jerusalem and Oxford, and for shorter periods to a great number of universities. His particular interest during the last years have been to analyse the development in prison figures in industrialized countries. He hosted a conference in Oslo in 1995 on this topic. He has also functioned as a member of the National Criminal Justice Commission in Washington, which recently published on report, "The penal war on crime" (Steven Donziger, ed.).

David Downes has been a member of the London School of Economics, Department of Social Administration, where he is now a professor, since 1963. He read History at Keble College Oxford, later undertaking his doctoral research in the Department of Sociology at London School of Economics. His thesis, published as *The delinquent solution* (1966), remains a classic in English criminology. He has also written *Gambling, work and leisure* (Downes 1976), *deviant interpretations* (Downes and Rock 1979) and *Understanding deviance* (Downes and Rock 1988). *Contrasts in tolerance*, a comparative study of penal policy in this country and The Netherlands is also a standard of English criminology. Throughout his career David Downes has worked with pressure and other groups with a concern for criminal justice – the Labour Campaign for Criminal Justice, The National Council for Civil Liberties, The National Association for the Care and Resettlement of Offenders, The Howard League and the Fabian Society being some of them. His current research is about social inequality and crime policy.

Frances Heidensohn is professor of social policy at Goldsmiths' College University of London. She read sociology at the London School of Economics and taught there first in the Department of Sociology (1964–70) and later in Social Science and Administration (1971–74). From 1974–79 she worked at the Civil Service College as a lecturer, then director of studies in social policy. In 1979 she moved to Goldsmiths' College where she became senior lecturer (1985), reader (1990) and was appointed to the chair of social policy in 1994. She was associate editor of the *British Journal of Criminology* 1983–93 and vice chairman of the Institute for the Study and Treatment of Delinquency. She has been involved in the NHS since 1982 and has chaired a health authority since 1992.

Simon Holdaway is professor of sociology at Sheffield University. He left school at 16 to join the Metropolitan Police Cadet Corps, serving as a police officer for 11 years. During his period of police service he was seconded to Lancaster University where he studied sociology and religious studies. After graduation he returned to the police and registered as a part time PhD student at the London School of Economics. In 1975 he was appointed lecturer in sociology at Sheffield University. He has researched the police extensively, focusing on the occupational culture of the rank and file and race relations within constabularies. Among his publications are, *Inside the British police* (1983), *Recruiting a multiracial police force* (1991), *The racialization of British policing* (1996) and *Resigners: the experience of black and Asian police officers* (Holdaway and Barron 1997). He has also researched the governance of the probation service and aspects of equal opportunities in different organizations. His present research is concerned with race relations within Metropolitan Toronto Police.

Richard Jenkins is professor of sociology at Sheffield University. Educated as a social anthropologist at the Queen's University of Belfast and the University of Cambridge, he has done field work in Belfast, the West Midlands area of England, south Wales, and western Jutland, Denmark. His general field of interest is the social construction of individual and collective identity, with specific respect to the transition from youth to adulthood; ethnicity, racism and nationalism; and disability, particularly learning difficulties and intellectual disability. He has also done research on moral panics about Satanism and black magic in modern Northern Ireland. Among his books are *Pierre Bourdieu* (1992), *Social Identity* (1996) and *Rethinking Ethnicity* (1997).

Ken Pease is currently professor of criminology at Huddersfield University. He has also held professorships at the Universities of Manchester and Saskatchewan, and was also head of the School of Sociology and Social Policy at Ulster Polytechnic and a principal research officer in the Home Office Research Unit. He has served on the Parole Board and has acted as consultant to the United Nations Crime Branch and the United Nations Drug Control Programme. His books include *The psychology of judicial sentencing* (Fitzmaurice and Pease 1986) and *Uses and abuses of criminal statistics* (forthcoming). Much of his recent research has concerned the phenomena associated with repeat victimization.

Robert Reiner is professor of criminology in the Law Department,

London School of Economics and director of its Mannheim Centre for Criminology and Criminal Justice. He was formerly reader in criminology at the University of Bristol and at Brunel University. He has a BA in Economics from Cambridge University (1967), an MSc in sociology (with Distinction) from the London School of Economics (1968), a PhD in Sociology from Bristol University (1976), and a postgraduate Diploma in Law (with Distinction) from City University, London (1985). He is author of *The politics of the police* (1965; second edition 1992a); *The blue-coated worker* (1978); *Chief Constables* (1991); and editor of: *Beyond law and order* (Reiner and Cross 1991); *Accountable policing: effectiveness empowerment and equity* (Reiner and Spencer 1993); *The Oxford handbook of criminology* (Maguire, Morgan and Reiner 1994; second edition 1997); and *Policing* (1996). He has published over 100 papers on policing and criminal justice topics. He is editor (with R. Morgan) of *Policing and Society: An International Journal of Research and Policy*, and was review editor of *The British Journal of Criminology*. He was president of the British Society of Criminology from 1993–96. His present research is a study financed by the Economic and Social Research Council analysing changing media representations of crime and criminal justice since the Second World War.

Paul Rock is professor of social institutions at the London School of Economics. He was formerly director of the School's Mannheim Centre for the Study of Criminology and Criminal Justice, editor of the *British Journal of Sociology* and review editor of *the British Journal of Criminology*. He obtained a BSc from the London School of Economics (1964) and a PhD (1970) as a student at Nuffield College, Oxford. He has been a visiting professor at Princeton University (1974–75); the University of California, San Diego (1972), Simon Fraser University (1976) and the University of British Columbia, (1976); a visiting scholar at the Programs Branch of the Ministry of the Solicitor General of Canada (1981); and a fellow of the Centre for Advanced Study in the Behavioural Sciences, Stanford, California (1996).

He is author of a number of books, including *Deviant behaviour* (1973a); *Making people pay* (1973b); *The making of symbolic interactionism* (1979); (with David Downes) *Understanding deviance* (revised second edition 1995); *A view from the shadows: the ministry of the solicitor general of Canada and the justice for victims of crime initiative* (1987); *Helping victims of crime: the Home Office and the rise of victim support in England and Wales* (1990); *The social world of an English Crown Court* (1993); and *Reconstructing a women's prison: the Holloway redevelopment project 1968–88* (1996). Jointly and singly, he has edited a comparable number of books. He is currently working on a history of the origins and development of practical and political responses to the aftermath of homicide.

Clifford Shearing was born in Durban, South Africa, where he went to school before moving to a farm near Underberg in the Drakensberg Mountains to work as a farmhand. He later returned to Durban to do an undergraduate degree at the University of Natal. On completing his degree he got a job as a Personnel Manager in a large rope and matting factory where he survived for less than a week. He returned to the University to work as a research assistant on a study of blood donation. Following this he completed an honours degree in sociology at Natal. He then moved to Canada where he joined the Centre of Criminology at the University of Toronto as a Junior Research Fellow. He proceeded to complete a masters and a doctorate in sociology at the University of Toronto. He is presently director of the Centre. With the political changes in South Africa in the early 1990s he returned to Cape Town for two years and worked through the University of the Western Cape to set up a programme of policing within its Community Law Centre. This programme grew into the Community Peace Foundation where he was first director and then academic director. He continues to be associated with the Foundation and undertakes work under its auspices. His scholarly research has focused on issues of control, power and government which he has explored through studies of strategies and institutional arrangements used to provide security. The primary exception to this focus was a brief period in which he undertook research and writing on stuttering (he is a stutterer). He continues to use policing and regulation as an empirical site through which to develop theory.

Elizabeth A. Stanko, reader in criminology at Brunel University, holds a PhD in sociology from the City University of New York (1977). She taught for 14 years at Clark University, Worcester,

Massachusetts, taking her position in the Law Department of Brunel University in 1990. Her interest in criminology was sparked during her undergraduate sociology degree, awarded by Lehman College, CUNY in 1972. Serendipity fostered her interest in violence. She has been active in the debates and dialogues about violence and gender since the late 1970s and she has published extensively in this area of research, including, *Intimate intrusions: women's experience of male violence* (1985) and *Everyday violence: how women and men experience physical and sexual danger* (1990a). She has recently been appointed as research director of the Economic and Social Research Council's Programme on Violence.

CHAPTER 1

Thinking about criminology:
"Facts are bits of biography"

(Lafferty 1932)

Paul Rock and Simon Holdaway

We embarked on editing this book in the belief that there is an
important gap in the writing on criminological theory, and that doing
something to fill that gap could help to improve understanding of the
work of criminology and criminologists. Let us explain.

Descriptions of scholarly activity tend to differentiate sharply
between paradigmatic revolutions and normal science (Kuhn 1970);
between brief bursts of innovation and longer periods of intellectual
quiescence; between work that is analytically-driven and work that is
driven by policy problems; between the theoretical and the empirical;
the pure and the applied; the abstract and the concrete. In many of
these dichotomies there appears to be a presumption that theorizing
should be regarded as a pursuit apart, as a special, self-conscious
process that strives logically and systematically to propound general
principles that are, in effect, removed from our knowledge of the
small, messy, immediate, here-and-now world of the senses. It is as if
theory and theorizing may be found only when they parade quite
explicitly under those names; that there can be no theory where
none is intended. We exaggerate, of course, but not by very much.
Academics are quite prone to make use of such contrasts for
didactic effect.

At first glance, there is good evidence for the existence of those
polarities within criminology. It is to be found in the university
courses and academic textbooks specifically dedicated to theoretical

1

and applied criminology and in the ways in which people label their own practices, even though criminologists may well move in and out of different positions at different phases of their careers.

Criminology has a tacit division of labour. There are a number of scholars, a small minority perhaps, who self-consciously call themselves *theorists*, and some of those theorists engage in intellectual exegesis (Nelken 1994). If much mundane criminology may be described as a set of scientific ideas about lay ideas, as an interpretation of the way in which people construct lines of action and reasoning as they make, break and enforce rules, these exegetical theorists work at a greater distance to supply ideas about ideas about ideas (Schutz 1967). They explain, elaborate, criticize and compare their own and others' published thoughts about the world of crime with the aid of larger analytical principles derived from theories of ontology, epistemology, politics, law, sociology and philosophy. In so doing, they meet the besetting problem that, contemplating large, transcendental questions about the explanation of social life, they may be prompted to move so far away from a consideration of the empirical events of crime and social control that their very identity as criminologists will become threatened. They may come to proclaim, for example, that they are "against criminology", or that they wish to deconstruct criminology, draft an obituary for the sociology of deviance or announce that feminism of Marxism or ethnomethodology has supplanted criminology (Cohen, S. 1988; Smart 1989; Sumner 1994). The significance and interest of crime and control can become quite diminished by the grand schemes they propound. So it was that radical criminologists could once state:

> Criminology and crime are not central disciplines for radicalism – indeed … a concern with criminology will fade as a radical analysis is achieved … the idea of a radical criminology is not possible in principle … Marxism as a form of theoretical system specifies its own objects of analysis and … those objects are not crime or law, but the mode of production and the form of social relations in general … Marxism, by the analysis of the relationship between and within social formations, includes and subsumes (logically and empirically) the analysis of crime and law in these more general concerns (Bankowski, Mungham and Young 1977).

Or a phenomenologist could write:

> In thinking out of deviance ... I would treat it as a theoretical imperative the very thrust of which would be to overcome it as a descriptor. In this way we could then turn away from constitutive and arbitrary judgments of public rule breaking as deviance towards the concept of rule itself and the dialectical tension that ruling is a subject surely more central to the fundamental practice of sociology where men and sociological speakers are conceived as rule makers and followers. What is now the sociology of deviance might then be pushed to the margins of sociological discourse as a museum piece to be preserved perhaps as that antediluvian activity which sought to show oddities, curiosities, peccadilloes and villains as central to sociological reason (Phillipson 1970).

In thus condemning criminology, such exegetical theorists confront a dilemma; they must either effectively relinquish criminology and turn wholeheartedly to grand theory or else quit grand theory and return to criminology in a more accommodating frame of mind. Consider the later careers of Taylor, Walton and Young, the authors of an important, early piece of grand theorizing, *The New Criminology*. Taylor and Young are no longer grand theorists and Walton is no longer a contributing criminologist (Taylor, Walton and Young 1973). Either way, it is clear that there are intrinsic incompatibilities between grand theory and criminology (and between grand theory and any other empirically-based "sociology of" a particular area for that matter). An empirically-based discipline is inhospitable to great speculative systems.

Other theorists may be recognized by their attention to large, general issues of substance. They may, for instance, touch on the criminological consequences of globalization and the weakening of the power and authority of national governments to enforce law; the social implications of femininity and masculinity for understanding crime as a predominantly male pursuit (Messerschmidt 1993); rituals of "reintegrative shaming" as strategies of control (Braithwaite 1989); and the new geographies of crime and control that are beginning to reveal how space may be mapped into areas of safety and danger in a new political economy of risk (Davis 1990). They have accomplished much that is promising, although it is not grand theory in the sense that C. Wright Mills would have known it (Mills 1959.) It is certainly not conducted on a plane so lofty that it leaves empirical issues behind. On the contrary, it is informed, as almost all criminology is informed, by the need to understand social problems that have been defined, as it were, from below and substantively, by the "facts" of crime, law and law enforcement, and not by criteria emanating from some metaphysics above. Such theoretical criminology frequently borrows from intellectual developments in criminology's parent disciplines, and from sociology above all, putting them to work (and sometimes enlarging and transforming them) in its own special terrain of crime and control. It is that willingness to deploy theory in the service of ambitious empirical enquiry, not a difference of intellectual kind, that confirms this second, grounded form of work as theorizing.

There are other criminologists, and they are almost certainly the great majority, who would hesitate to call themselves theorists at all, who might feel somewhat uncomfortable talking and writing in an overtly theoretical vein, who would profess to be content exploring practical problems without aiming overmuch at abstraction, generalization and analytic formality. Their ambivalence about, or, at worst, dismissal of theory seems to have gained ground within criminology. The measurement of outcomes, a concern with the immediate symptoms of malfunctioning policies, evaluation research, and an acceptance that the agenda for criminological research can be set by criminal justice professionals and their representative associations, seem to have become distinctive of the discipline.

In part, those criminologists' hesitation may stem from an acquaintance with the fate of the grand theorists who have not survived, whose efforts at theorizing effectively disabled them as criminologists. But they have other motives for hesitation, and it would be best to list them because it is the work of these criminologists which largely concerns us in this book. For practical reasons, we shall draw on British examples although very similar arguments could be advanced about work in North America and Australasia.

Criminology, like many another branch of learning, is what David Downes once called a *rendezvous* subject, that is, it is defined principally by its focus upon an empirical area, not by its allegiance to any particular theory or set of theories. It is and must be crime that gives criminology its peculiar territory and programme; around crime have clustered a mélange of interested disciplines – sociology, psychology, law, statistics, medicine, physical anthropology, social anthropology, psychiatry, economics and others. Each discipline has turned some part of itself on the study of crime, and that part has been changed in consequence. Work has been affected by the special analytic problems and rewards of studying crime (things are learned in criminology that may not be discovered elsewhere), by the growth of local intellectual traditions (thus, sociological criminology is different in some important particulars from the sociology of development or employment), and by the interaction of intellectual disciplines inside the confines of criminology. Sociological crimin-ology in Britain, for instance, was much influenced by the encounter that took place in the 1960s between the symbolic interactionism of the "labelling school" and the applied statistics of Leslie Wilkins, an encounter that was to culminate in ideas of "deviance amplification" and "moral panic". In its turn, the idea of moral panic came to meet radical Marxian political economy in the analysis of a "mugging" conducted by members of the Birmingham Centre for Contemporary Cultural Studies and social history in Pearson's account of the endless rediscovery of the moral problem of delinquency (Becker 1963; Wilkins 1964; Cohen, S. 1972; Hall et al. 1978; Pearson 1983.)

Yet it is its empirical core that continues to lend coherence and cohesion to criminology, and we have argued that criminologists cannot wander away too far from that core before they risk forfeiting their claim to be criminologists. Whatever they might do in the name of theory, there can be no forsaking the empirical centre of criminology. The fact that criminology is an ineluctably empirical discipline serves as a constant check and brake on its propensity to theorize.

Those empirically-grounded traits have been reinforced by the peculiar demographic structure of the population of criminologists, at least in the United Kingdom. One of us conducted two surveys of British criminologists in 1987 and 1992 (Rock 1988). It became evident that the people practising criminology form a fairly homogeneous group, most (well over half) having attended university in the late 1960s and early 1970s before moving into their first professional positions. They were, in effect, members of what Rock called the "fortunate generation", people who had entered the discipline en masse some 20 years ago when higher education expanded in the wake of the Robbins Report, and they have stayed to dominate it ever since, no longer young Turks, but middle-aged (*Higher Education Report* 1963).

British criminologists were trained in only a few institutions (40 per cent took their postgraduate degrees in four institutions: the Universities of Cambridge, Oxford and Sheffield and the London School of Economics); they work in a geographically small country; they are not numerous (some 400 attended the biennial meeting of the British Criminology Conference in 1995, for instance); and they are quite similar in age (their modal age was 46 in 1992, 68 per cent being older than 40) and gender (80 per cent are men). They are, in other words, a cohesive group marked by what Alison Young once called an "internalized cosiness" (Young 1990) They work together, write together, teach one another, attend the same conferences and seminars, sit on the same committees and editorial boards, befriend one another and sometimes marry one another. An academic publisher specializing in criminology once remarked to one of us that British criminologists were regarded in his profession as a rather special group: "They all know one another!"

There have been marked consequences for the production of criminological knowledge. Most members of the fortunate generation underwent a critical phase of theoretical discovery together as graduate students in the late 1960s and early 1970s. They experienced that decade as volatile, exciting and argumentative, marked by abundant conferences, publications and public disputes, and by the formation of the National Deviancy Conference at York University in 1968 (Cohen, S. 1971). It was a decade in which they sought self-consciously and perhaps a little too confidently to establish the proper intellectual character of British criminology, sometimes in opposition to what were conceived to be the orthodoxies of an older, more conservative group. They issued manifestos, intellectual revolutions and bold new syntheses (Taylor et al. 1973; Smart 1977). What they established then, the British variants of symbolic interactionism, Marxism, phenomenology and feminism, came to inform much of their subsequent work. In effect, they succeeded in fabricating the visible theoretical structures which would serve them for the next 20 years. They might well have subsequently modified their ideas, but they acted as if they had undertaken an appreciable public work of theorizing and felt little need ever to undertake it again quite so energetically. Calm followed storm in a manner quite characteristic of spates of intellectual innovation in universities, and theorizing declined (Crane 1972). By the early 1990s, moreover, the law of diminishing marginal intellectual returns was at work. A compact, reasonably intimate network of professional criminologists in Britain and elsewhere had come to know each other and each other's work well enough not to have to repeat commonplace arguments again and again. After all, there was very little profit in reiterating points that were perfectly familiar to their audience. Many of the theoretical issues that had once exercised them had grown stale and criminologists no longer wished to debate them. Indeed, after a while, resurrecting arguments about basic ideas is quite likely to be construed as divisive in a small professional world where people are obliged to co-exist: instead of quarrelling, members may prefer simply to avoid one another or refrain from discussing contentious topics (Becher 1989). The effect has been that the theoretical has tended to become what ethnomethodologists would call "indexical", it is now thought to be so well-known that it can be silently presupposed as the unstated context of meaning which frames communications between informed insiders. It is as if theory had been partially submerged, becoming so taken for granted that it has attained the status of common sense. It may be presumed to exist but it is no longer clearly visible to the untrained eye.

If the theoretical elements of much criminology became more discreet and private in the 1980s and 1990s, it was otherwise with those that were empirical. A triple onslaught of brute facts accelerated the movement of the discipline away from abstraction and general systems, particularly in England and Wales. First there was the steady and spectacular increase in crimes recorded by the police. Until the 1920s, the annual recorded level was under 100,000; it rose to 500,000 in 1950, to 1,600,000 in 1970, 2,500,000 in 1980 and 5,400,000 in 1992 (Digest 2 1993). To be sure, the criminal law, public reporting and police recording practices, technologies and public sensitivities all changed during that time, but it could not be contested that the problem of crime had become much more serious and perturbing. One criminologist, Reiner, remarked in 1995:

So many people are rightly more cautious nowadays about saloon-bar pontifications on rising crime and declining moral standards. Yet even with appropriate warnings most commentators – and I certainly include myself – feel this time things are really different. We are caught up in a long-term expansion of crime and disorder, which has been with us for nearly forty years, and which has intensified greatly in the last year and a half (Reiner 1994).

What acted forcibly to impress that problem on the criminological and political consciousness was its sudden and shocking dramatization in the 1980s when rioting in Brixton, Toxteth, Bristol, Haringey, Meadowell and elsewhere seemed luridly to advertise the precariousness of order, law-observance and legitimacy in the inner city. The 'rioting was so spectacular, so well-publicized, so fiercely debated, so freighted with meaning about crime and control, that it demanded attention from criminologists who seemed at first rather ill-prepared to understand quite what had happened. It was as if the empirical world had rudely forced aside older preoccupations and ideas. It clamoured to be heard.

The second set of facts followed close on the heels of those riots (Rock 1990). Attempting to mount a visible response to the Brixton disorders of 1981, and emulating the National Crime Surveys that had been pioneered in the United States in the 1970s, the Home Office inaugurated in 1982 what was to become the first of a succession of victim surveys, that is, random household surveys designed to estimate the volume, distribution and character of crimes experienced by a population during the previous year. It is difficult to exaggerate the impact that they achieved. The new facts they supplied were intellectual anomalies that could change minds. Initiated to measure crime more efficiently, to "improve the criminal justice data base" as officials put it, the surveys came to furnish data on an ever-widening range of criminological problems and on the geography and demography of risk, in particular. It became clear that the volume of crime is even more massive than the official figures suggest: the informal estimate now given by the Home Office is that some 19,000,000 offences are committed annually, three times the sum recorded by the police (although all such estimates inevitably confront metaphysical questions of definition about what crime may

8

be and how it can be identified and counted). It became clear too that the suffering imposed by crime is felt most acutely by those who are already beset by other problems, by poverty, discrimination, inadequate housing, unemployment and the like. Crime, argued David Downes, is a regressive tax on the poor. Criminologists, and radical theorists above all, began to heed that suffering, shedding notions which some had once held. There was talk about victims when there had been none before. Radicals found it harder to treat crime as an ideological distraction or mystification devised to deflect popular anger away from the real problems of capitalist society (Pearce 1976). Crime was no longer treated as a form of class justice. Quite revealing was the recantation by the "left" criminologists, John Lea and Jock Young, in 1984, a year after the publication of the first British Crime Survey:

> There was a schizophrenia about crime on the left where crimes against women and immigrant groups were quite rightly an object of concern, but other types of crime were regarded as being of little interest or somehow excusable. Part of this mistake stems ... from the belief that property offences are directed solely against the bourgeoisie and that violence against the person is carried out by amateur Robin Hoods in the course of their righteous attempts to redistribute wealth. All of this is, alas, untrue (Lea and Young 1984; 262).

The third fact was the research environment generated by successive governments professing practicality, efficiency and value for money. It was not easy to secure state money to underwrite criminological theorizing in the latter half of the 1970s and the 1980s. Perhaps it has never been easy to do so. But funding bodies such as the Economic and Social Research Council and the Home Office in England and Wales, and their counterparts elsewhere, came increasingly to be directive and interventionist, no longer content simply to accept the academics' own judgements of what work was adequate and important, financing what they conceived to be worthwhile, research that was deemed to be "policy-relevant" and "methodologically-sound". All the while, a growing proportion of criminologists were becoming increasingly dependant on soft money, obliged to work on short-term contracts to supply research to order for government departments, statutory agencies and voluntary organizations, and they were quite emphatically not paid to theorize.

It was predictable that a dialectic came into play. An empirically-focused questioning disclosed issues that prompted yet more questions, making the empirical ever-more intriguing as the collective attention of criminologists was turned towards its exploration, as criminologists thought about each other's work, and conducted their own work in turn. In competent hands, problems of multiple and repeated victimization, the links between crime and routine activities, and relations between the police and public, actually began to acquire interest and importance (Cohen and Felson 1979; Smith, D. 1983; Forrester et al. 1988). There was a hastening of the eclipse of theoretical by empirical problems, leading some to talk about a crisis in criminology and of "the need to strengthen [the] theoretical and conceptual aspects" of the discipline (Heidensohn and Silvestri 1995).

But it should not be supposed that theory has disappeared altogether. Quite the reverse. Much has simply become tacit, a matter of private reflection, lying below the surface of even the most empirical reports. Solitary theorizing inevitably exercises criminologists as they go about the difficult business of selecting problems, consulting publications, formulating methodologies, putting questions, considering answers and phrasing analysis. How else could it be? Atheoretical enquiry would lack structure, coherence, boundaries and aim. It could not be reported to others for want of an interpretive frame.

Theorizing persists, but it has become subterranean in the work of the many criminologists who are simply too pressed, too preoccupied with the empirical, too dependant on funding agencies uninterested in speculation, or too jaded to conduct their theorizing publicly and as a main pursuit.

We had little prior idea of the character of that subterranean theorizing. It was quite possible that lack of critical exposure and systematic cultivation might have rendered it comparatively raw, naïve and underdeveloped even to the criminologists who espoused it themselves. However, it was equally possible that empirical criminologists were indeed quietly constructing interesting systems of thought, that they were moving from one project to another in an analytically deliberate manner, and that, indeed, their entire life work could be seen as a theoretical enterprise undertaken, as it were, *sotto voce*. We did not know whether subterranean theorizing was transparent to the criminologist in whose mind it unfolds (so transparent, indeed, there could be some incredulity at its opaqueness to others), or whether it would demand determined excavation and reflection before it assumed a presentable shape (after all, as Graham Wallace once asked, "How do I know what I think until I see what I say?"). Some parts of subterranean theorizing might prove to be original enough to warrant inclusion in the canon of criminological writing, or they might be little more than a tired echo of theories better expressed by those who worked professionally as theorists. They might possess the same forms and motifs as conventional theory or be quite different in kind, reflecting their peculiar bonds with the disciplines and exigencies of empirical enquiry. Broaching those questions and bringing theorizing to view could not fail to be fascinating and useful.

In effect, *Thinking about criminology* is an attempt to discover more about the hidden life and variety of that subterranean criminological theory. We hoped to retrieve what might otherwise have been lost through want of a public voice, and we did so in the expectation that that theorizing might be just as telling as its more obvious and self-promoting counterpart. We hoped perhaps to learn more about subterrranean theorizing as a practice, demystifying theory and, indeed, criminology at large, by showing how it could be seen as a pragmatic, grounded and contingent process very different from the impersonal, abstract and highly formal business of scholarly reasoning that it is often represented to be. We were intrigued to learn about how such theorizing might intertwine with the subjective and the biographical; how it might mediate professional careers; to what degree, in other words, it was a symbolic extension of the criminologist's self. At the very least, we imagined that the chapters of *Thinking about criminology* would make a contribution to the history of ideas.

To that end, we approached a number of criminologists who have already made their mark, who would not probably conceive of themselves chiefly as grand theorists, and who reflect something of the intellectual diversity of the discipline. We invited contributors to

> stand back and reflect upon the ideas that underpin their work ... to describe their more general theoretical pre-

occupations, examine what bearing they have had upon their work, and speculate about how they might evolve in the future. The outcome [we hoped] would not only lay bare the more or less tacit theorising that we believe informs current criminology, but also make a useful contribution to the history and study of the discipline.

Such an invitation could never have led to artless analysis: theorizing had to emerge in the very act of reflection, and it was inevitable that the autobiographical would have been theorized, just as the theoretical would have become autobiographical. What is represented here is not the same as the process of theorizing actually experienced in situ by working criminologists. It could never have been so. Ideas cannot remain unformed as they are brought to consciousness and translated into writing. But the empirical criminologist's experience of theorizing probably could never have been captured in its proper character. It is prepredicative, pre-reflexive, a result of immersion in the field. Those who allude to it sometimes speak of unplanned and ineffable shifts of understanding that defy description. A distinguished empirical criminologist, William Foote Whyte, once reflected:

> Probably most of our learning in [the] field is not on a conscious level. We often have flashes of insight that come to us when we are not consciously thinking about a research problem at all. These insights are more likely to come to the man who is absorbed in the field situation than to the one who is always going in and coming out in order to maintain his perspective (Whyte 1951).

The replies to our invitation have been revealing. The contributors to this book have been candid and considered in their writing, and we believe that they have furnished a valuable glimpse of the private life of theory. There have been such accounts of the research process in the past, but almost none of theorizing as a practice (Bell and Newby 1977). *Thinking about criminology* discloses how many empirical criminologists do conceive themselves to be theoretically-driven and how theory informs almost all they do. Criminology represents the resolution of analytic problems carefully phrased by their authors, even though those problems may not always be recorded in their entirety in subsequent written reports.

The book also reveals how, in a number of instances, that theorizing came to represent the evolving resolution of issues central to the self, how early were those issues implanted in the criminologist's mind, and how bound up with his or her identity and life-project. Intellectual, political and professional careers seem frequently to run in parallel. And the book further discloses how theory can mediate a self and a self-theory, how gender can be critical to the feminist and political economy to one alert to the politics of crime, different selves, in effect, emerging from different conceptions of theory, reminding one of how the pragmatist, Peirce, once claimed that 'my language is the sum total of myself' (Peirce 1934).

One principal conclusion is that there may often be only a slight existential gap between the seemingly impersonal domain of research and the personal domain of the researcher. The one refracts the other: observer, observed and the process of observing being importantly fused. In this sense, research and writing may be read as an unfolding, visible and objective documentation of the private subjectivity and experience of the scholar. Experience in its pre-reflexive state, Dewey remarked, is "double-barrelled in that it recognizes in its primary integrity no division between act and material, subject and object, but contains them both in an unanalyzed totality" (Dewey 1929). Research, of course, is not merely an unedited outpouring of subjectivity. It has its controls, professional demands and public forms that give it shape, discipline and anonymity, that estrange it from the person who conducts it, but it is also more intimate than many may have supposed. Perhaps that is why scholars are so very sensitive to negative criticism; it is not just an alienated product of labour that is condemned but part of what William James would have called the material self, the self realized in the form of a written artefact.

CHAPTER 2

Theorizing – sotto voce

Clifford Shearing

Only one more word concerning the desire to teach the world what it ought to be. For such a purpose philosophy at least always comes too late. Philosophy, as the thought of the world, does not appear until reality has completed its formative process, and made itself ready. History thus corroborates the teaching of the conception that only in the maturity of reality does the ideal appear as counterpart to the real, apprehends the real world in its substance, and shapes it into an intellectual kingdom. When philosophy paints grey in grey, one form of life has become old, and by means of grey, it cannot be rejuvenated but only known. The owl of Minerva takes its flight only when the shades of night are gathering (Hegel 1836:XXX).

Introduction

In their introduction to this edited collection, Paul Rock and Simon Holdaway contrast theorizing as it is normally understood – that is "intellectual exegesis" of the grand sort – with a more subterranean understanding grounded in, and essential to, practice. They remark that while many criminologists have eschewed conventional theorizing, they have very often engaged in theorizing in this second vein. They talk about this as a "theoretical enterprise undertaken, as it were, *sotto voce* ..." They suggest that what might at first blush look like a lack of interest in theory might indeed be theorizing in a different voice, undertaken behind the scenes so to speak, yet moving forward in a deliberate and systematic manner from project to project. This understanding conceives of theoretical work as a commonplace activity. Theory is the set of claims about the world that we use to go on from one space–time moment to the next. Theory makes living possible. It orders our world by making that world visible and available to us as a terrain within which we can act. As we act through our theories in this way, we reflect on them and modify them. Theory building happens incrementally and continually. It happens in and through scholarly projects, but it also happens in whatever we do. Essential to this view of theory is a notion that it not only provides a way of understanding the relationship between events in the world, but that it provides for a way of seeing the world in the first place – it makes "reality" thinkable. Action requires theory. What distinguishes the theories we build as scholars from those we all use to get on with the business of living in our everyday lives is the rigour we seek to achieve in terms of explicitness, parsimony, agreement with logical requirements such as internal consistency, the testability of the predictions made when a world is made visible, and so on.

Fundamental to this view of theory and theorizing, as I understand it, is a recognition that ways of seeing are not themselves strictly testable, as they make the testable world visible. Whatever world is made visible, however, is certainly consequential for how we go about organizing our lives. How we "problematize", "how very different things in the world are gathered together, treated, characterised" (Foucault 1988:17) makes a difference for the way we live. This is not to say that there is not a reality out there, but that we always see this world through a lens, a lens that is shaped by our location, both culturally and much more personally.

This idea is nicely illustrated by the story I have encountered about how the people of the Americas did not see his ships as ships when they first saw Columbus approach, because this possibility did not exist for them. Closer to home is the example of the lens provided by the ladder of evolutionary progress that encourages us to view, what Darwin termed, "descent with modification", as "a linear sequence of advancing forms, shown either globally, running from an amoeba to a white male in a business suit ... or, more parochially, as moving from a stooped ape to an upright human" (Gould 1996). This imagery that shapes the way in which we interpret the evidence of modification is, as Gould (1996) has noted, not limited to popular culture, but has fundamentally shaped the development of evolutionary theory.

This view of theorizing challenges the theory–practice dichotomy at the same time as it personalizes theory-building by locating it in our cultural and idiosyncratic experiences. It regards theory as rooted in our life experiences, experiences that create our lenses, and it is our lenses that pose the questions and the problems that our theories seek to address.

For me, and I do not want to suggest that this is or should be true for everyone, the most exciting theoretical moments occur when someone's experience allows them to challenge taken-for-granted ways of seeing and to imagine and propose new ways of asking questions. Thomas Kuhn (1970) contrasts such paradigmatic shifts to "normal science", in which one works within, and elaborates upon, a way of seeing. These shifts challenge established ways of seeing and identify worlds that our previous lenses have overlooked. Again, Gould instructs:

> I have often had occasion to quote Freud's incisive, almost rueful, observation that all major revolutions in the history of science have as their common theme ... [t]he dethronement of human arrogance from one pillar after another of our previous cosmic assurance. Freud mentions three such incidents: We once thought that we lived on the central body of a limited universe until Copernicus, Galileo, and Newton identified the earth as a tiny satellite to a marginal star. We then comforted ourselves by imagining that God had nevertheless chosen this peripheral location for creating a unique organism in His image – until Darwin came along and "relegated us to descent from an animal world". We then sought solace in our rational minds until, as Freud notes in one of the least modest statements of intellectual history, "psychology discovered the unconscious" (1996:17–18).

Theoretical work of this sort identifies the way the world is typically conceived, recognizes that it can be seen differently, and then seeks to show how and why this is a useful thing to do. Doing this is not only theoretically exciting, but it is also a lot of fun. This form of theorizing requires, in Elkins' (1995:4) terms, that we discover what is "already happening, but virtually no one has noticed because discussion relies on a vocabulary appropriate to an era now ending rather than one that is being born or created or constructed". In my experience, it is very often through the inductive emphasis central to subterranean theorizing that we suddenly see what the "lens of common concepts" (Elkins 1995) has obscured, and then discover a conceptual scheme appropriate to it. Such breaks are often heavily dependent on figurative imagery that is deeply personal.

Criminology is a wonderfully rich arena for theorizing in this way, because it has been and continues to be a place within which different ways of seeing are juxtaposed. This is so because, as Rock and Holdaway note, criminology is a "rendezvous" subject where people from a variety of disciplines meet. What they meet about, for the most part, is security. They come together to think about how it is threatened, how these threats are to be thought about, what is being and can be done to manage them and above all, how all this is to be made thinkable. As I have just suggested, for many of us who rendezvous in this way, the *crime* in criminology is emblematic in the same way as the *pot* in pottery is. Security is what clay is to a potter, and like the many, many potters who do not make pots, there are many criminologists whose work extends beyond crime.

How does one see differently? How does one see anew? Hegel's metaphor about the owl of Minerva that takes flight only after the world over which it will fly has taken shape is instructive. Our theories make it possible for us to see and shape a world, but the world they shape can, and does, out-run them. To see it, we must escape our theories. Those who do so are often marginal, or out of place in some way, and it is their idiosyncratic vantage point that provides them with the standpoint they need to see what others overlook. This is the point at which the personal becomes the theoretical, the point at which biography becomes important.

The poetry of the personal

Like many – perhaps most – people, my life has been shaped by contingencies in the form of opportunities that once taken, have set me on a course that I could not have imagined, let alone have planned. But, of course, contingencies alone do not shape our lives. Our decisions to take one wind rather than another set the angle of our sails. While I have often presented the decisions I have made as rational choices, after weighing the pros and cons of each, when I am honest with myself, I know that this is seldom the case. My life, in most of its aspects, including my work as a scholar, has been moved more by inner muses and passions than by rational calculation. Like most people, I think, these "spirits" have emerged out of poetically charged experiences that have shaken me. Such moments are turning points, the figurative markers, in the narrative we construct as "our life". They are our poems, and it is these poems that lie at the root of our theories.

I grew up as a white child in a well-to-do family in South Africa where I spent my teenage years focused on horses – caring for them, schooling them, jumping them and so on. At one point I became convinced that I wanted to be a farmer, and when an acquaintance I had met through riding offered me and my best friend the chance to come and work on the farm he ran with his wife, we jumped at it. I became a cowboy – up at dawn, on my horse most of the day, and in bed early. I also came to see apartheid as a political system for the first time, its racism, and more importantly, the extent to which my perception had been shaped by apartheid as a way of seeing. Before the year was out I was fired for "inciting the natives to rebellion", and given two hours to leave the farm and make sure I did not return. On the farm, as I herded cows, built fences, ploughed fields with a team of oxen, and shared my life with my fellow farm labourers, I had realized for the first time how I had unthinkingly inhabited a world that now looked quite different to me, how my consciousness, that I thought was somehow mine, had been shaped and structured by a political apparatus. This mechanism was not centred in the capitals of Cape Town and Pretoria, but was alive, well and flourishing on this farm – it had not been just the farmer who had fired me, but apartheid. Its agents, I realize, were everywhere. I was, and continued to be, an agent of apartheid, as was the farmer

19

and all who worked there. How could this be? How did this happen?

My time spent in the glorious mountains of the Drakensberg, riding out into the veld each morning, cultivated a passion for beauty and grandeur, but it also created a passion to understand how I had become so thoroughly a person of my time and place, and the nature of the power that first shaped me and ultimately moved against me when I dared to question it. I also wondered how I, who had been so much a part of apartheid, had questioned it at all. I had seen differently because I had come to see through other eyes. On this farm I learnt both at first hand, and through others, what it is to stand apart, albeit just a little. With time I realized that at the heart of my questions was the issue of agency, the problem of "going on". How had I gone on? How had others? How was it that we all went on in much the same way? How did all our goings on fit so as to produce and reproduce apartheid? How had every one around me, white and black, male and female, become so fully and completely part of the system? What was the system, and, finally could it be beaten?

Rendezvous with theorists

I wanted, for the first time, to go to university. Once there, while my examination results showed little evidence of it, I had a wonderful time thinking and learning and arguing and arguing and arguing. In my second year I discovered sociology, and with sociology, Durkheim. What a revelation and an inspiration – one of those magnificent experiences in which things fall into place. Here was someone who spoke about the system, not in those words, but in words that resonated and made sense – words that enabled me to give some shape and meaning to the system. Durkheim spoke of a social world that was "out there", that could be studied and understood, and above all, a world that shaped individual consciousness. My problem in understanding the system had been that I was operating within a deeply rooted set of assumptions that saw people and their thoughts as basic, fundamental and as always coming first. Durkheim turned this on its head.

I was, by this time, familiar with the social contract theorists and particularly Hobbes' view of the "state of nature" made up of conscious thinking people existing in an anomic pre-social state. Durkheim's work represented my first and most influential encounter with a deep and thorough going critique of the humanist idea that our thoughts, and the actions that follow, spring fully-formed from within us, that this "within" is separate from the world "out there", and that language was a tool we used to communicate our private interior world with others in our exterior world. Through Durkheim, I glimpsed at a whole new set of possibilities, a whole new way of looking at "the self", at the inside–outside distinction, at the sources of action, and at almost everything I had assumed I knew about what it was to be human. "The system" was not just the government, or some set of politicians, or even a ruling class, it was "the social world", and this world reached deep into lives and indeed into their psyches. It was a consciousness, a sensibility we breathed and breathed life into, every moment of our lives. Durkheim was charting a new terrain of human conscious-ness. Durkheim had identified what was for me a new way of making the world thinkable and a new set of questions, a new problematization. What he identified for me was a quest for a very different conception of human agency, and for a conception of power appropriate to it. This quest that began for me on a dusty road outside a farm with my bag at my side waiting for a bus, was now a scholarly pursuit. Today, although I have travelled a long way, spending time with the Chicago School, the labelling theorists, Husserl, Schutz and Weber, again in studies at the New School for Social Research in New York, Garfinkel and his students, Foucault, a whole range of feminist thinkers, and some wonderfully imaginative thinkers who are exploring Foucault's thinking on governance, the quest remains essentially the same – how are we to understand human agency and its articulation with power? My teaching has sought year after year to follow the twists and turns of this big question, and to identify new insights and new ways of exploring it. After Durkheim I had, and still have, as many queries as ever, but I had found a productive way of thinking about them.

Shortly after Durkheim, I was introduced to Weber by a wonder-ful teacher, to whom I owe an enormous debt, Hamish Dickie-Clarke. With Weber there was a similarly revealing experience. What interested me about Weber were his reflections on method and the differences between him and Durkheim. Weber argued that to comprehend we needed to do more than to be able to explain through the discovery of laws from which predictions could be made, we also had to understand the meanings of events through a process of Verstehen – "the interpretation of action in terms of its subjective meaning"(Weber 1964:94). I read the thinkers Weber drew upon, like Dilthey, and was persuaded that understanding was as central as Durkheim's call for studying the social world as a world of things for providing accounts of human action and interaction. While I saw mainly differences between Durkheim and Weber when I first encountered them, as I have thought more about language, and more broadly, discourse, as ways of seeing and being, these theorists no longer seem so different. It is the sensibilities that Durkheim's "collective consciousness" makes possible that Verstehen seeks to grasp, and that make such an understanding possible. It reveals and depends upon what James Boyd White (1985) in his wonderful book, *When words lose their meaning*, calls a "culture of argument". White captures Weber's understanding and relates it to Durkheim when he talks of reasoning as "a way of making sense in an actual situation in a particular culture" (1985:22). He captures and extends this relation when he writes: All human experience is at once unique and collective: during a war, a child dies of cancer, an old man of a bad heart; another baby is born; a scientist discovers a new compound and the infidelity of his wife; a soldier is killed in an accident, another by the enemy; one man's bravery leads to his death, another's to the rescue of a friend, and so on. The full reality of these ties is not the story of the war only, or of those private events only, but of all of them together, seen and felt simultaneously from every human point of view (Durkheim 1985:57–8).

It is Durkheim and Weber who provide the early sign posts along that hot, dry Drakensberg road. Since these authors, there have been many others, and each time they have provided for different ways of seeing the excitement of refiguring the old, and thereby glimpsing a new that has been the same.

Policing and what that implies

Almost all my empirical work, with a few exceptions like my exploration of stuttering, has been about policing. Why? Certainly not because I was drawn to it for some deep compelling reason. Like criminology it is something I fell into for contingent reasons. But once I got up and looked around, I realized it was not a bad place to have fallen. This surprised me as I had, as a sociology under-graduate, sought to steer clear of anything that bore any relationship whatsoever to "deviance". As I was, I felt marginal enough as a stutterer not to want to flag my awkwardness by studying deviance or the processes surrounding it. Fortunately for me circumstance encouraged me to decide otherwise.

The place into which I had fallen was the Centre of Criminology at the University of Toronto, an institution that has proved to be a wonderful, wonderful place to work – a research institution with an academic culture that has always been full of interesting scholars, has been remarkably free of political in-fighting, has been exceptionally open to diversity and, accordingly, that has always encouraged its members to trek off in whatever direction they wanted. When I began work at the Centre as a staff member I looked around for an "open" area in which to work. No one at the time was working on policing, so I decided to explore it. When I began this work, policing meant, as it still does for most people, police work and so I looked towards the police. The central concern at the time was what police officers did and how they did it. The crucial question within this focus was police discretion, in particular, the extent to which what the police did fitted with what the law said they should do. Packer's due process/crime control distinction was central to these debates. The focus was entirely on the state, on political authorities and on their agents, the police.

I engaged with this line of thinking, but its focus on the state worried me from the outset. My South African experiences had encouraged me to question state-focused understandings of power and the system, and I worried about doing that here. Police was surely not all that policing was about? There were few apartheid police at Drakensberg, yet my actions and thoughts had been thoroughly policed. Where were the parts of the policing system. How was policing embedded into their lives. So, I looked for people beside the police who were engaged in policing, who were part of the system. No one else, or almost no one else, who wrote about policing seemed concerned about this, despite the fact that one of the statements most associated with the police was the Peelian line that the police were the public and the public were the police. What must have been there was being "obscured by the lens of common concepts" (Elkins 1995:4). The system (I was already worried about this notion, but more suitable concepts were not available to me), I began to realize, included all those people who called the police for assistance. The police were almost completely dependent on calls for service from citizens who acted as unpaid informers. Although they were volunteers, not only were they doing police work, but doing work and detection that was regarded within the police as high status work. The plot soon began to thicken. As I looked and read further, it became apparent that police detectives did remarkably little detection, and comparatively speaking, detected practically nothing. The real detectives were citizens who detected problems, and for the most part, provided the so-called detectives with the intelligence they needed to solve them.

This shook me and excited me. Although it took me longer to figure out than it should have, I began to realize that I, and others, had the topic wrong. The topic I should be studying was not police work but policing, as a generic activity. This proved to be a fundamental intellectual turning point that has shaped the way I have thought since. What this said to me was that the established sociological focus on institutions, roles and positions was very limiting. Not only was this a problem, but this was very much a Durkheimian limitation. Durkheim's social world was a normative reality made up of rules for doing things. These rules were organized into roles, and these roles were associated with positions that people took. To study the social world, one needed to study its institutions, that is, the packages into which roles and positions were organized. If one was to study politics, one studied political institutions. This was true of every other area of sociology. To study education, one studied educational institutions, and so on for medicine (hospitals), work (businesses) and policing (police departments). This was a pretty blinkered way of seeing.

So what was the alternative? If we had been thinking in terms of nouns, perhaps it was time to focus on verbs. Instead of starting with institutions and moving from them to activities, perhaps one should begin with the activities, with the practices. It meant making policing the focus, not police work.

This account, even though I am trying to keep this analysis as close to my thinking at the time as I can now, is still far better developed than my thinking was then. What I did realize, very clearly, was that to study policing one should study more than police work. This led me to follow in a path that others were just beginning to tread, to explore detecting outside of the police. The research task I identified as a way of doing this was to study calls for police service, a piece of research that led to a monograph titled *Dial-a-Cop*. This was a small step, but it was a challenge to the central assumptions underlying what came to be thought of, very appropriately, as Police Studies. It argued, as much implicitly as explicitly, that policing as a set of assembled practices that took place across, rather than within institutions, should be the focus of research on security. This was, I now realize, an early though unrecognized Foucauldian turn, that argued that "theory attends too much to institutions, and too little to practices" (Gordon 1991:4). This caused questions about agency to resurface and how various practices that were not explicitly part of the system nonetheless contributed to it in an organized and systematic way.

This research also led me in another direction that also took up the question of agency. I did the data collection for the study by sitting alongside complaint officers and listening in on calls to the police through a headset plugged into their lines. This meant that besides listening to calls, I spent a lot of time listening to police officers as they talked back and forth with one another and who thought, as I did at the time, that my interest was in what the complainants had to say. I soon discovered that their chitchat was also very revealing. Here, right before my eyes, was Durkheim's "social world" at work. Here was a "collective conscience" playing itself out.

The police literature on discretion saw this culture as a rogue set of instructions, a set of recipe rules that were a source of police deviance to the system's instructions as they were spelt out in the law and departmental regulations. The police culture was conceived as resistance to power, not as part and parcel of the way it was exercised. My life experience, my farm and my Drakensberg road, had made me deeply suspicious of this way of thinking, this way of making up the world.

As I sat listening to police officers talk I became increasingly uncomfortable with another feature of this way of thinking, namely, the notion that culture should be conceived as a set of instructions for doing things. I heard little said that took the form of recipe rules in the same way, for I had heard little on my farm that sounded like a cookbook for doing apartheid. These police officers were not guiding each other on how to "go on" with rule talk. They were not, to jump ahead in my thinking, "governing through rules" (this phrase adapts Jonathan Simon's lovely expression "governing through crime").

Finally, there was a third issue that began to nag at me as I did this research. The police literature adopted what I also took to be a Durkheimian tendency to see the police culture as directing the actions of all police officers in much the same way. Those officers who were socialized into the police culture would obey its dictates and deviate from the rules of the law and the police department. Those who did not would not be committed to the rules and act according to their dictates. Apart from the fact that this reasoning tended in practice to be tautological, as it was "deviant" action that was most often cited as evidence of the culture, the "black box" feature of this argument bothered me. There was little room here for police officers interpreting rules and reacting to them. Where was Weber's insistence that "explanation requires a grasp of the complex of meaning in which an actual course of understandable action takes place?" The established analysis remained at the institutional level of roles and positions, albeit deviant ones.

Each of these concerns arose as a result of a questioning of the expectations that flowed from the reigning approaches being taken at the time. These questions arose in part because of what I observed at the time but they also arose because I saw this world through the lens of my personal, idiosyncratic experiences. Without this under-lying scepticism I doubt that I would have raised the questions I did. I would have been unlikely, or so it seems to me, to have the assumptions and vocabularies of the literature.

While I vaguely recognized this at the time, the implications of this have become clearer to me with time. Had I not felt uneasy about the direction taken by the literature right from the start, the lens of its common sense is likely to have led me to see the world of policing in a much more conventional manner, and I would have engaged in Kuhn's "normal science". My scholarship, then and now, was and is abnormal in this specific sense, because my scholarship has ultimately been grounded in the personal – a personal that has created a standpoint within which the Anglo–American academy is just different enough for me to feel uncomfortable with many established ways of seeing.

The questions I have just outlined about the way in which power, agency and Durkheim's concept of the "social" are thought about have continued to capture my attention (and others as Foucault's thinking has become more widely known), and have shaped my choice of research topics and the questions I have raised within each project. Each research endeavour has provided an opportunity to revisit these queries about sociological theory and its account of human agency and the exercise of power. I have sought to bring to each project my emerging understanding of how these questions should be put and the answers I have developed to them on the basis of prior research and the thinking of others.

With each project I have sought to develop better answers, and more importantly, better questions. Whether my research has been about stuttering, the regulation of financial markets, the police, private security or the implications of neo-liberal rationalities for the security of poor people, the theoretical questions have been framed around the same central issues, and the quest for theoretical clarity has been much the same. Indeed, the specific topics could have been very different – housing, health, urban life – any empirical focus would have served as well. The criminological topics I have engaged in, however, have served my country road well. Each project and piece of writing have provided an opportunity to return to that road, with its trees, its fence post and its views of the mountains. Within this consistency there has been constant change and challenge, for these issues are, at least to my mind, big questions that can be returned to afresh again and again. With each return there are new "Ah ha's", new challenges and new excitement.

In returning to these questions, I have found it particularly useful to do so in the company of others. I have found that thinking aloud in conversation, and collecting material with others and eventually writing with them, is enormously productive. I have been favoured by the company of wonderful co-authors. A central feature of the fun of scholarship, for me, has been the excitement of working ideas through with others with whom one shares enough to work together, but with whom one disagrees enough to have plenty to argue about. (I recognize that the tone of this section and much of the chapter is unfashionably content and up beat, well, that's just the "way it is".)

Private governments and action at a distance

One of the most lasting, resilient and productive research partnerships has been with my colleague Philip Stenning. Our work has pursued two related lines of enquiry. The first has sought to extend and develop the insight that it would be useful to focus analytic attention on practices and then explore where and in what contexts these practices occur. Beginning with a focus on policing, we soon realized that police officers were not the only specialized agents who did policing, and that police organizations were not the only institutions in which such persons were located. We noted that many of the things that police officers did within state structures were also done by others within corporate structures. As we looked around us, we noticed that there were security guards and private investigators everywhere. Yet we, like most people, had overlooked them.

This led to an exciting series of inquiries that began with simply going out and trying to count the people employed within private security organizations as guards and investigators and documenting what they did. From this modest beginning, we were led beyond this relatively visible presence of specialized, but non-state, security agents, to an exploration of the way in which policing functions were imbricated with other practices. The critical moment within this line of inquiry, for me, occurred on a trip to Florida with my daughter, Renee, and a school friend of hers during their winter school break. I had been looking forward to snorkeling in the Keys and enjoying the sun and the sea. They were happy with this, but they also wanted to visit Disney World, and so off we went with me trailing rather reluctantly along. From the moment we tuned into Disney Radio as we approach this World, and were directed to our parking lot, lights began to go on, first a few, and then an explosion of them.

Policing, I discovered in Disney World, was everywhere and it was everybody's business. There were few people around whom I recognized as security officers, but there was much security. Here were the contours of the amorphous system I had glimpsed in the

Drakensberg mountains, and had so much difficulty grasping, laid out before me with remarkable clarity. Here, policing was not owned by one particular set of people, by security officers or police officers, but it was done by everyone – by visitors, by parking attendants, by robotic images and messages, by Mickey Mouse and Donald Duck, by everyone and everything. In Disney World, everyone was responsible for security – in Pat O'Malley's terms, everyone was "responsibilized".

The possibility of embedding policing throughout the social fabric is no longer news, though it certainly was to Stenning and me at the time. Today this possibility has been extended to governance more generally and has become a central feature of a move to "reinvent government" (Osborne and Gaebler 1993) that is re-shaping the way in which governance takes place from Australia to South Africa. Disney's way of doing things is now being embraced everywhere. This is a theme that President Clinton has returned to again and again recently, and was a central focus of his second inaugural address.

Today we can declare: Government is not the problem and not the solution. We the American people are the solution … As times change, so government must change. We need a new government for a new century, a government humble enough not to try to solve all our problems for us but strong enough to give us the tools to solve our problems for ourselves, a government that is smaller, lives within its means and does more with less …The pre-eminent mission of our new government is to give all Americans an opportunity – not a guarantee, but a real opportunity – to build better lives … And we need a new sense of responsibility for a new century. There is work to do, work that government alone cannot do: teaching children to read, hiring people off welfare rolls, coming out from behind locked doors and shuttered windows to help reclaim our streets from drugs and gangs and crime, taking time out from our own lives to serve others … Each and every one of us, in our own way, must assume personal responsibility, not only for ourselves and our families but for our neighbours and our nation (*New York Times*, 21 January, 1997: A12).

A feature of the governance of Disney World that was novel to us when we identified it has now emerged as increasingly common-place – its instrumental focus expressed a concern with risk and risk reduction, and there was an associated focus on what victims, and potential victims, could do to reduce the risk of victimization. This feature – which our research on private security revealed was a pervasive characteristic of private governments – has developed as a widespread phenomena that is pervading the mentality of state governments.

What was overlooked has been identified as a fundamental feature of political rule. What continues to be obscured, even in the emerging governmentality literature, is the emergence of private governments. Not only are the ruling mechanisms of political authorities located primarily within state structures giving way to expanding networks that permit rule to take place at a distance (Rose and Miller 1992), but the authorities of governance are proliferating to give birth to what Stenning and I termed in the mid-1980s a "new feudalism", made possible in part by the emergence of "mass private property" of which Disney World was but one example among many (Shearing and Stenning 1983).

Liberty, equity and democracy

While this has not come out explicitly in this story to this point, my work has typically blended descriptive with normative questions, not simply because of my desire to play a part in shaping how we, as human beings, can and should live, but because scholarship generally, and criminology in particular, is deeply imbricated with politics. A good illustration of this is the opportunity I took a few years ago to actively engage in the transformation of South Africa. This occasion arose as a result of an invitation I received from Dullah Omar, the South African Minister of Justice, to assist in stimulating a debate around police reform within South Africa, and to participate in a variety of ways in policy development around policing. This request opened up a rich set of opportunities that has enabled me to draw on the concepts I have been developing and to extend them in unanticipated ways.

One of these issues has been the topic of private governments and the inequalities of services and autonomy they have introduced. The emergence of such governments as a routine feature of our lives raises critical issues with respect to democracy, equity and liberty that are only just beginning to be recognized and have received very little theoretical attention. For some people, generally the well-to-do, the emergence of private governments has brought a number of benefits. They, for example, can, and for many people do, provide for more direct and participatory forms of control over the way in which their lives are governed. One need only reflect upon the implications of those who live in, and help manage, the gated communities and gated cities that are springing up all over the world to get a sense of this. Within these feudal-like domains, people often enter into contracts that determine the extent to which their liberties will be infringed and the extent to which their person and collective resources will be devoted to the provision of security. For others, very often the less well-to-do, this is not the case, both because they do not have the same degree of access to the terrains of private governments, and because the contracts available to them are likely to be less advantageous. Consider, for example, the prisoners in Britain are now being accorded the "opportunity" to enter into "contracts" to choose the nature of their confinement (Garland 1997).

This issue of access to contractual governance, and the terms of such access is a matter that Mike Brogden and I (Brogden and Shearing 1993) have argued is critical to the nature and future development of South African policing. In exploring this issue, we drew upon the work of Richard Ericson as I did on the nature of police culture. In developing the critique I have touched on above, Ericson and I have argued that police culture should be understood as a set of mythical stories not unlike fairy tales. David Dixon (1995:63–4), in commenting on this work, describes our conclusions succinctly in these terms. They latch on to the stories which all police researchers have heard, laughed at, been bored by and repeated, but have regarded as essentially trivial ... It is through telling and hearing them that officers know how to act. Importantly, this account provides for agency: officers are not "cultural dopes", but make choices in performing police work.

Brogden and I argued on the basis of this argument that as the occupational culture within the South African Police was deeply rooted in the mythical foundations of Afrikaner culture, it would be very difficult to transform. This encouraged us to challenge the efficacy of the conventional strategy of reform which was, and is, to find ways of modifying the police occupational culture through training. We argued that while this strategy should not be abandoned it should be complemented by one that seeks, where possible, to shift the institutional location of policing away from the police.

I was fortunate enough to be in a position to explore this idea in practice as a member of a panel of experts set up to find ways of policing demonstrations during the South African election period. The panel accepted the above analysis and proposed that the primary responsibility for the policing of demonstrations be given to demonstrators. The normative device used to promote this was to establish a provision whereby organizers of demonstrations were required to develop plans for the policing of demonstrations. The outcome was that many hundreds of marshals, belonging to political parties, were trained to police demonstrations, and the record now shows that they did so with remarkable success. The South African Police were still involved, but the need for them was greatly reduced, and they now had to co-ordinate their plans with those of the demonstrators who were now in a position to audit what the police planned to do as well as what they did. This did not change the police culture, but it did constrain it. Here theory shaped a politics of policing and helped establish a crucial condition for the development of a democratic politics within the country.

Conclusion

The point of these very personal reflections has been to explicate the process of theorizing Rock and Holdaway identify in their introduction when they explain that the theoretical explorations described in essays in this volume reveal how theorizing came to represent the evolving resolution of issues central to the self, how early were [sic] those issues implanted in the criminologist's mind, and how bound up with his or her identity and life-project. There may often be only a slight existential gap between the seemingly impersonal domain of research and the personal domain of the researcher; the one refracts the other, observer, observed and the process of observing being importantly fused. In this sense, research and writing may be read as an unfolding, visible and objective documentation of the private subjectivity and experience of the scholar. I hope that they also throw light on the *sotto voce* nature of much theoretical writing within criminology. My intention has been to use my story to learn more about subterranean theorizing as a *practice*, "demystifying" theory and, indeed, criminology at large, by showing how it could be seen as a pragmatic, grounded and contingent process very different from the impersonal, abstract and highly formal business of scholarly reasoning that it is often represented to be. Theorizing can, and does, take place outside of explicitly theoretical writings and can, and in my view should, take place in ways that are closely tied to empirical digging and political practice and contestation. The theoretical, the empirical and the normative are, at their best, mutually reinforcing activities.

CHAPTER 3

Making the invisible visible in criminology: a personal journey

Elizabeth A. Stanko

A personal introduction

I am a 46-year-old, North American born in the mid-west of the USA, educated there and in New York City; a sociologist who self-identifies as a criminologist. I started by working on two large scale criminological research projects in New York City, taught for 14 years in a sociology department in a small private liberal arts university in Massachusetts, and took my first job in Britain in 1990 as the convenor of an MA in Criminal Justice in a Law Department, where I am now.

I am female, white, middle class, heterosexual, a mother, non-disabled, non-religious, and self-identify as a feminist. I am usually classified by others as a so-called radical feminist – which means that I supposedly place the primacy of women's oppression above the myriad of oppressions. My problem is that I care too passionately about the issue of violence against women. Sometimes it is difficult to separate my personal commitment to minimizing the damage of violence from my professional role of analysing that damage. Occasionally, for example, I find myself over-emoting on podiums, pleading for better understanding or *common sense* about how institutions, laws, and social and criminological theory serve as mechanisms to make violence and brutality invisible, especially that committed against women by men. I put my concerns into practice, establishing with others a refuge for battered women in Worcester,

Massachusetts. Today I am more of a theoretical strategist, plotting ways to introduce feminist perspectives into popular discourse on a variety of topics in criminology. It is for this reason that I actively appear on a variety of media in the UK – radio, TV and in the press. It is for this reason that I try to write in an accessible, jargon-free way.

The work

As the dog's body of two research projects at the beginning of my career, I experienced so-called criminal justice in action. Court houses, prisons, probation offices, judges' chambers, prosecutors' offices, police stations and therapeutic residential houses all became familiar places from which I gathered statistical information about the processing of criminal cases. These early experiences served as dislocaters – sites where I observed firsthand that practice was very different from theory. I was an adept chameleon, able to blend into so many different settings. These were valuable lessons for the budding ethnographer. The one irritant I seemed to experience was the constant reminder that I was female. Cat-calls and sexualized comments came during my visits to prisons (both inmates and staff joined in), judges' chambers, prosecutors' offices, police stations and professional meetings. The criminal justice business was, and still is, dominated by men. I usually fended for myself, aided by my quick wit and my occasional angry retort.[1]

Early influential theorists

Key theorists in my development as a sociologist and criminologist were Erving Goffman (1963), Harold Garfinkel (1967) and Richard Quinney (1970). Quinney's (1970) *The Social Reality of Crime* alerted me to two sociological processes at work: 1) crime was a social construction; 2) there were alternative standpoints from which to view crime as damaging to society. Quinney, as both teacher and advisor, supported my growing impatience with the daily operations of the criminal justice system. Because my full-time job during my graduate studies took me into courts, prosecutors' offices and probation departments across New York State, I could see (and to me experience) first-hand the process of how various actors within the system made sense of their work. Such sense-making was rarely documented in the criminological literature of the early 1970s.

My own training for examining common sense was fostered by the intellectual traditions of ethnomethodology.[2] I characterize my approach as studies of the "taken-for-granted". Any analysis of police and prosecutors as key participants in the criminal justice is also an examination of their social knowledge. Such knowledge of prosecutors and police officers is firmly embedded in the "deeply ingrained institutional character of the decision-making processes" (Emerson and Paley 1993:246).

The production of this knowledge, and of legal fact-finding or evidence, suggested Cooney (1994) recently, is located in "who people are" as social beings. Garfinkel (1967) alerted me to the "omnirelevance" of being a man or a woman, with judgements of one's performance rooted in the wide, and varied, expectations of gender. All of this takes place within complexities of negotiating personal, institutional and socially-ordered power (Smith, D. 1990).

What I documented those 20 years ago in New York County Court – the significance of gender/race/class/intimacy in cases of violent assault, rape and robbery – still has salience today. My own ethnographic work was intended to articulate the then radical politics implicit in Quinney's theoretical approach, using the methodological approach of those who observe everyday life. My doctoral thesis, *These are the cases that try themselves* (Stanko 1977) was a study of the Manhattan district attorney's complaint assessment procedure. After exclusive access to New York's district attorneys' (DA) discretionary decisions about felony cases through 13 months of fieldwork, I described the DAS' assessments about the seriousness of violent cases, locating victim credibility as central to the determinations about seriousness of the offence (interesting, as I look back on it, my focus on the phenomenology of violence began then, when I looked at robbery, assault and rape) (Stanko 1981–2). In an era when greater professionalism meant greater efficiency, prosecutors were promoting their expertise in separating *real* crime from *technical* crime (Bumgartner 1993). The fact that the process of doing so often rested on the perceived social respectability of victims was rendered invisible to the process.[3]

My curiosity about how police make decisions about serious crime was sparked by my analysis of prosecutors' work (Stanko 1981–2). How did these actors in the criminal justice system apply their organizational knowledge to serious cases (Stanko 1981)? So for three months, I observed police of the 9th Precinct (famous for the opening shot of the TV series *Kojak*). My observations included ride-alongs, as well as time spent in the so-called arrest processing room within the stationhouse itself. But the team of officers I observed was also being watched, by the Internal Affairs Division – and during my fieldwork, half of the shift was arrested for robbery in the first degree, extortion and assault. Apparently, five officers *in uniform* had been robbing drug dealers – four cops were subsequently convicted. I witnessed the internal strife of rank and file officers; the stress they experienced from working in a dangerous, high crime area; and the solidarity which welded them to each other. These experiences grounded my later writing and research on the police, which were to happen over a decade later.

As I see it now, police or prosecutors make decisions about whether and how matters brought to their attention will be given access to redress in the criminal justice system. This is essentially a social decision about the provision of societal resources, masquerading as an objective, legal one. In a recent essay, Emerson and Paley (1993) discuss the nature of discretion. They suggest, "If we view discretion simply as decisions that are unguided by rules, we dichotomise decision outcomes into those that are in accord with the relevant rules and those that are not" (1993:245). Emerson and Paley argue for a richer, contextual approach, one which makes explicit the organizational knowledge which fills in what legal actors need to know about the routine matters coming to their attention.

I nestle my work on prosecutors, and to some extent on the police, within this study of the "taken-for-granted". My approach is compatible with those researchers who explore policing (Fielding, Holdaway, Manning, Van Maanen, Young, for example) and prosecutorial decision-making (Cooney, Emerson, Frohmann, Mather, for instance) through an ethnographic tradition. Ethnography displays the processing of criminal justice cases about violence which rests in the conceptual contexts of offenders', witnesses' and victims' social, situational and structural positions. It is well-documented, for instance, that the patterns of decision-making in criminal justice advantage those with greater social resources. It is this observation that leads Bumgartner to propose:

> How individuals fare in the legal system turns out not to be mysterious, and, what is more, not random. People enter the legal process with very different prospects, depending upon their own social characteristics as well as those of their opponents, supporters and the officials who deal with them (1993:157).

Goffman's (1963) *Stigma* inspired my analysis of the *in situ* assessment of character and witness credibility displayed by prosecutors and police. For example, during my fieldwork, a young couple was robbed at knife point in the lower East Side of New York. The prosecutor rated the robbery very seriously and had classified it as a first degree robbery for prosecution. The young man returned just after the case was classified, to inform the DA that he had been in the area to buy heroin. The DA recalled the papers, reclassified the crime, and thus the case proceeded as a less serious offence. Such dynamics in how DAs judged witness credibility could only be explained through an analysis which recognized the fluidity (and rigidity) of social identities, with credibility ordered hierarchically. Patricia Williams's (1991) *The Alchemy of Race and Rights* is a recent example of confronting the recalcitrance of racist/racism embedded in identities. In one chapter she describes being refused entry to a Benetton's in New York's Soho:

> No words, no gestures, no prejudices of my own would make a bit of difference to him [the sales clerk]; his refusal to let me into the store – it was Benetton's … He saw me only as one who would take his money and therefore could not conceive that I was there to give him money (1991:45).

DAs, judges, police and other actors within the criminal justice system are no different from that sales clerk at Benetton's.

I focus on this early period to highlight two points about my work; it could not have been done without some first hand knowledge of the criminal justice system in operation. Second, these experiences were my entrée to what I saw as unrecognized in making sense of routine criminal justice decisions. My professional task, as I see it, is to make visible that which is rendered invisible by organizational discourse, political rhetoric and silence about inequity in the criminal justice systems which are rooted in unfairness within democratic states (Phillips 1993).

What does this say about theory? While it is certainly possible to theorize about something of which one has had no direct experience, it is also very possible to silence accounts of phenomenon which are not compatible with the dominant political and academic discourse. If one believes that efficiency promotes more equitable justice, for instance, then one does not ask questions about the consequences of such efficiency for those seeking justice via the criminal justice system. If one chooses to ignore the human tragedies so often associated with redress in the criminal justice system, one chooses to ignore the contexts within which crime and victimization fester.

What I observed time and time again in the prosecutors' complaints room and on the streets with the police was that those with fewer resources – the poor, the homeless, drug addicts, battered women, non-white and non-English speaking people, and others – were less likely to have violence and other criminal matters considered an affront to society and thus prosecuted as felony crimes. What is prosecuted as felony crime often reflects violence fostered by these and other structural disadvantages (see Daly 1994). So the courts – and a great deal of police time – are occupied with the physical, emotional and financial inequality which exist in a seemingly open, free democratic state. Quinney's thesis rings true today as it did 25 years ago.

In comes the feminism

Within the last decade, I have illustrated the inequity of the criminal justice system through a dialogue with one (among many) contributor to systems of inequity: that is gender. This is perhaps the criminological work for which I am best known and which had an inauspicious beginning.

I had hoped to extend the insights of my doctoral research during my first year as an academic in Worcester, Massachusetts. However, I could not get firsthand material on the police, nor on the prosecutors there. I was refused access to the DA's office (no reason given). I was told by the then chief of police that he did not want to take responsibility for a woman riding around in squad cars (this was especially galling after my exciting times with the New York City police). But it was the mid-1970s, and feminist activism was strong in Massachusetts. I became involved with the rape crisis centre and, in 1978, founded a refuge for battered women along with other, mostly student, activists.

Through teaching a course on women and crime in 1977, I realized – as did many of my female cohorts in criminology – that there was a paucity of criminological work which featured women – or even which included women in their samples. I turned my interests to exposing criminology's neglect of women (Rafter and Stanko 1982; Stanko 1982). My own activism (praxis, if you prefer) continued; I was president of the Board of Directors of Daybreak, the refuge for women, so I learned about resistance in my own community to making violence against women visible. But it was my own struggle against sexual harassment which provided me with my everyday insight into the personal impact of structures which promote women's silence about violence and intimidation.

With no direct experience of men's violence, save the daily indignities and feelings of threat women routinely encounter (most people think that all radical feminists are just damaged women, see also Gardner's 1995 study of public harassment), suing my employer for failing to act when complaints about my (and others) sexual harassment were lodged, taught me more about mechanisms of silence and social control than any academic review ever could (Stanko 1996a). In a thoughtful and thought-provoking monograph, Kirsten Bumiller (1988) suggests that being a victim of discrimination is a collective phenomenon, a condition of the relationship between the powerful and the powerless. Power-lessness, she further opines, is not a *possession* of an individual, it is relational and socially constructed. In declaring victimization, an individual must stand apart from the collective experience and announce specific effects of unequal treatment. Asserting dis-crimination, as an individual claimant, means separating oneself from the collective inequalities and making a public declaration about the right not to be treated in such a way.

In demanding the right not to be sexually harassed, I was objecting to what had been and is considered to be routine: sexualized treatment of women at the hands of men. Many of us choose to find other ways of resisting and/or coping with the intrusion of men's sexualized comments. Liz Kelly (1988) speaks of how some of us minimize the violence we have experienced. Bumiller speaks of individuals becoming engaged in "a politics of survival – a battle designed to preserve the bare minimum of human autonomy" when one decides to cope individually without the assistance of a legal tribunal or collective or personal confrontation which might have served the purpose of validating an accusation of sexual harassment (1988:70). In an analysis of why people who identify themselves as unequally treated fail to demand redress, Bumiller proposes that anti-discrimination laws uphold the status quo of state power rather than support the claims of those harmed. Many feel ambivalent about asking the state for redress, because they feel they may be more harmed by the process of fact-finding. So too, we may doubt our own responses to felt discrimination, however hurtful and frightening these experiences might be. Should we feel aggrieved if we are just life as usual, which includes abuse? These personal insights, born from my own encounters with the legal system, continue to influence my own analysis of the processes entangled with victimization today.

Although my case was eventually settled out of court in our favour, I left the US on a sabbatical in 1982 for respite in London, with the intention of writing a book about violence against women. *Intimate Intrusions* (Stanko 1985) examined the mechanisms for maintaining and reproducing the invisibility of men's violence to women. Women's silences about abuse – fed by shame or self-blame, and the systematic denial of our experiences of abuse by the criminal justice system and other institutional means of redress, formed (and still form) powerful barriers to naming violence against women as a significant social problem. No doubt that is beginning to change. But it seemed to me then that so many were reaching out to rape crisis centres and refuges for help – and so few of us seemed to be successful in gaining access to the democratic system of redress – criminal justice. Where were our public grievances? Largely invisible.

My feminism comes to my criminology

It was in the early 1980s when my own work sought to make visible to traditional criminology the kinds of so-called crime which affected women's lives most: private violence. Take a look at criminology textbooks in the 1980s and you will see an emphasis on violence which occurs in public places. Random robbery, assault and rape dominate the literature. Yet feminist surveys, most notably that by Diana E. H. Russell (1982) in the US, documented the prevalence of violence throughout women's lifetimes. Most often, though, we experience this violence at the hands of relatives, partners and other men we know.

The British Crime Survey (BCS) influences significantly the debate about crime and victimization in Britain. I entered the fray by declaring that men's violence to women was not captured by the BCS (Stanko 1983). For instance, in the first BCS, only one attempted rape was reported to the interviewers, who questioned only women about sexual offences (approximately half of the 10,905 respondents to the first BCS). Did this finding make sense, given the virtual obsession we have about our sexual safety (Gordon and Riger 1988)? How is it even possible to speculate about violent crime in general if so much of it fails to come to the attention of the police and survey interviewers – a point which was especially stressed in the feminist literature about battering? I queried the ability of such surveys to capture adequately women's experiences of violence (Stanko 1988), especially when our reported fear of crime was and is consistently captured by crime surveys to be at levels three times that of men's. To speculate about fear of crime without a sensitivity to gender was – and is – surely a mistake (Stanko 1995b).

Policy-driven, administrative criminology flourished in Britain during the 1980s (Downes and Morgan 1994). In Britain, there was a sense that somehow the right policy could impact crime and the so-called fear it caused. Police sold themselves as experts in crime management but found they were faced with a crisis in confidence over the handling of public disorder. During the 1980s, I became interested in two areas of such policy: the conceptualization of fear of crime (Stanko 1987; 1988; 1990a; 1990b) and the policing of domestic violence (Stanko 1989; Stanko 1995b).[4] But rather than provide an artificially simple solution to these dilemmas, I chose instead to highlight the complexities. Needless to say, I was never funded for any of my work during the 1980s.

Theoretically, I was interested in contributing to the feminist enterprise which articulated women's everyday lives. I explored women's anxiety about and experiences of men's violence as one window of that articulation. I was very much influenced by the growing debates in feminist legal theory, most notably the contribution of Catherine MacKinnon (1979, 1982, 1987, 1990). My support in Britain was provided by the British Sociological Association's Violence Against Women Group, formed after the 1985 BSA meetings in Hull. (I lived a trans-Atlantic existence, migrating permanently in 1990.) Three women in particular influenced my own thinking: Rebecca Dobash (see Rebecca and Russell Dobash (1979, 1992), Liz Kelly (see, in particular, Kelly 1988) and Jill Radford (1987, 1989) on issues of women and violence, and Frances Heidensohn (1985, 1992) on the possibility of being a feminist in the criminological enterprise.

Questions I raised about fear of crime resonated questions raised by feminists about the nature of work, children and childbearing, madness, history, to name only a few. One of my original contributions to British criminology, I feel, is persistently drawing attention to the gendered nature of fear of crime. I proposed in 1987 that women's fear is founded in our fear of men. My in-depth interviews with men and women on both sides of the Atlantic examined the untidiness of concepts such as *fear of crime* (Stanko 1990a). I tried to make sense of the experience of anxiety of crime in a jargon-free way. I argued against characterizing women as defeated by fear, living under virtual curfew (Crawford et al. 1990); we are not always afraid, nor do we live lives in constant anxiety. But some of us are very fearful – and that fear is often (but not always) a direct or indirect result of experiences of men's violence – for both men and women. Most of us though have found ways of coping with potential violence and threat.

So, in the spirit of my earlier ethnomethodological training, I sought to confront criminological common sense – that *fear* of *crime* was related to public danger. This did not make sense to me; as women, we are most likely to encounter danger from men closest to us. This paradox, to me, must be theorized as an example of gender relations rather than as linked to an understanding of traditional

44

crime (see also Young, V. 1992). Interestingly enough, Rachel Pain's (1993) recent doctoral thesis suggests that women do report fearing unknown men more than known men, despite experiences to the contrary. Could it be that the very discourse about crime itself acts to privilege a fear of the unknown (Tuan 1979; Sparks 1992)?

My analysis of the crime prevention advice flowing forth from the Home Office and elsewhere explores this very discourse about crime. Police and other presumably authoritative advice seized upon the notion of fear of crime, especially ours, characterizing it as somehow unrealistic and unwarranted. In examining the volume of crime prevention literature produced during the 1980s, I found that people – especially women – were portrayed as incompetent in avoiding crime. *Practical ways to crack crime,* the flagship publication of UK Home Office crime prevention public relations office, highlighted women's fear in particular. We were advised to keep our handbags clasped to our bodies, to put petrol in our cars, to avoid dimly-lit alleys, as if these were revelations in safekeeping (Stanko 1990a, b). But as criminologists we insisted on maintaining a rigid separation between fear of the so-called private and the fear of the so-called public. Crime prevention advice fed into this separation.

My use of a gender-sensitive analysis continues to question the entire domain of the work exploring fear of crime. What is a gender-sensitive analysis? It is one which unpicks a male/female standpoint from which generalizations about crime, fear, victimization and so forth flow. This does not mean that there is unity in a so-called female perspective, nor one in a so-called male perspective. As Dorothy Smith suggests, speaking from experience "was a method of speaking" (1990:2) which grounded women's worlds in our experiences of it. I simply did not believe criminological analyses which were so insensitive to the primacy of sexual safety in our lives, and eschewed women's understanding of safety from a discussion of fear of crime. If our fears were so unrealistic, were not also men's, who by all official accounts, failed to report feeling concerned about crime themselves? To understand how men located themselves within continuums of safety (non-fear), men (in all their variations) should be studied for how they accomplish their masculinities through their own safekeeping practices. Smith (above) proposes that the sociologist "explores and explicates the actual determinations and organisation of the actualities of people's experienced worlds" (Smith, D. 1990:3). Being male and being female, to me, is a master narrative which colours all experience. Fear of crime, as a criminological conceptualization, is one of the best venues from which to explore how masculinities and femininities continue to be accomplishments of daily routines.

The second policy area I engaged with in the 1980s is the policing of domestic violence. Police attempts to assuage our fear included the targeting of the provision of services to women who had been raped or battered. I found I had something unique to offer the debate. So I returned to my lessons about police and policing which began on the streets of the 9th Precinct. To me, the salient features of the police as an organization were: its thoroughly masculine nature (Heidensohn 1992); its internal cult of rank and file resistance to management and loyalty to each other (Van Maanen 1973); its locus of discretion in street-level policing (Skolnick 1966); its belief in its own myths (Manning 1993; Crank 1994; Rawlings 1995); and its sense of mission (Reiner 1992a). Given the above, my scepticism about the adaptability of this organization to the needs of women informed my inquiry (Hanmer et al. 1989; Stanko 1989; Stanko 1996a).

While actively involved in the debates about the policing of violence against women, an exploration of policing and police strategies to minimize local violence attracted my first research funds (Stanko 1991). A study of how local police respond to requests from the public about threat and violence in Tower Hamlets and Liverpool was cast as a practical approach to address the problem of repeat victimization. Through a focus on violent crime, we discovered that many people were indeed asking for police assistance. In both areas, the kind of violence for which police were called was the kind of violence that I suggested was largely confined to silence: racial harassment and domestic violence. I learned that the dominant form of violence people attempt to find redress and respite from is the kind of violence for which police action cannot guarantee protection.

The lessons of this work were applied to a study of how local police and the local community collaborated to find a common definition about what constitutes threats to community safety and order (Dixon and Stanko 1993, 1995). We were given total access to one police division in London Metropolitan Police and explored their implementation of a form of community policing called sector policing. As much of the research on community policing suggests, there was a continuing search to discover what the so-called community *wanted*. Typically, those who failed to or were excluded from participating in the wish list about community safety were the very people who were most heavily in need of such assistance, or those who were most likely to come to the attention of the police. This study allowed me to begin to make problematic the theoretical link between the nature of policing and the desire for police protection in so-called democratic states.

In many ways, my work on violence against women and the nature of policing lead me to classic questions within criminology: what is the nature of social order? what is crime? what is the relationship between state ideology and the provision of public services (social policy)? is it possible to minimize the harm individuals experience from crime without altering the structures fostering and festering inequalities? Theorizing about power, its abuses and its uses, and the recurrence of inequity as a systematic feature of oppressions leads to my current work on crime and violence as accomplishments of doing masculinities.

How did my work on the police tie into my interest in gender? The link was twofold: silence and invisibility. These two processes which excluded men's violence against women from the criminal justice system also effected the way police conceptualized racial violence and community safety. The theoretical link goes something like this: Police, while promising equitable redress to the public, benefit from the failure of victims to report violence. Finite budgets would be very stretched indeed if the crime survey estimates of three-quarters of those experiencing violence suddenly turned to the police for assistance. This failure of victims to report, in turn, contributes to the invisibility of the pervasiveness of violence. When women in England and Wales began to contact the police about domestic violence matters, as they did in the past few years, reported violence rose. But the media coverage focused on the increase in violence as a decline in civility rather than an increase in reporting. We continue to treat violence as if it is a random occurrence, a bolt out of the blue (Stanko 1990b).

Reducing fear of crime, plus the fear of sexual, physical, racist or homophobic violence are the very sites where police promote their role as experts in public assurance (Stanko 1995b). Just as women's silence is a true measure of police lack of capacities to prevent such violence from occurring in the first place – violence against women is a measure of women's structural position – so too is the silence of people subjected to violence and abuse because of race, sexuality and disability who also seek redress from the criminal justice system. Police can rely on inequality to keep the demands upon them limited and to claim competence when they are in fact really relying on the personal resources and networks of social support, which all the research confirms women and others victimized use to find so-called protection. The fact that people are calling the police for protection problematizes the confidence people have in the police providing protection.

One final word about my work. During the last five years or so, I have begun to ask questions about masculinities and men (Stanko and Hobdell 1993; Newburn and Stanko 1994; Stanko 1994). The focus on men prompts me to examine my work on and about us as women in a different light. While I still firmly believe that we are structurally subordinate (with violence as one of the features of enforcing that subordination), I have benefited from explorations of masculinities, in a way which allows me – as a socially-positioned woman–feminist – to ask myself questions about my assumptions about femininities (see also Simpson and Elis 1995). I will address this in the final section about the future. In the next section, I would like to explore the theoretical importance of feminist criminologies for the study of social theory, crime and criminality.

Feminist critiques of criminology

What do social theories about gender, the processes of engendering, and the interactive dynamics of gendered performances tell us about crime, criminology and criminal justice? While I still feel strongly that feminist critiques within criminology continue to be marginal to the wider discourse of the discipline,[5] there is no doubt that feminists have challenged criminology's very core concepts. By asking questions about violence to women, for example, we ask questions about the definition of social order, crimes, violence and the state's response to offending and to those victimized. Yet there remain thorny and contentious issues within the explorations of gender and crime (Simpson and Elis 1995). In this penultimate section, I would like to explore the contribution of feminist criminology leading us to these current dilemmas, which will be addressed in the final section of this chapter.

Asking questions about women and men

Critical questions about gender, crime and criminality came to be asked by women and a few men who entered academia as scholars of crime during the so-called second wave of feminism in the 1970s/ 80s. Heidensohn (1968) wondered why there was no concern about the glaring gender differences in recorded criminality. Klein (1973) demonstrated the biological essentialism of theorizing about women's offending. Smart (1976) added her voice to this enterprise, with caution, "I hesitate to add to a body of literature that might be used to identify or discover another 'problem', to create another 'moral panic' " (1976:xiv). Nonetheless women like myself who wished to study criminology insisted that in doing so we would *at least* try to add women into the debates. Describing over two decades of contributions is not the scope of this chapter – there are now volumes of books exploring women and crime (see also Heidensohn 1994 and this volume). The point is that many of us contributed to the social theory of crime through our own concern about the treatment of women in wider society.

The debates about women's criminality, women's victimization and their handling by and within the criminal justice system flow through the theoretical and methodological developments within feminist theorizing (Daly and Chesney-Lind 1988; Gelsthorpe and Morris 1988; Simpson 1989). Feminisms are crucial to our theorizing; our theorizing is crucial to our understanding of the *praxis* of feminism (Ramazanoglu 1989). That is, if our ultimate goal is to minimize the impact of oppressions, then our theorizing should contribute creative ways of doing so. Crime and criminal behaviour says something about societal harms; feminist criminologists, as feminists, are concerned with changing society for the better in at least some respects, so feminists must assume that they have an adequate understanding of what is wrong with existing societies, and of the consequences of pressing for specified changes (Ramazanoglu 1989:44).

But did the development of feminist criminologies significantly alter the criminological paradigms which we criticized for not taking women on board? Here I am not so sure. I raise this because as social theorists we inevitably bring our own cultural baggage to our theorizing. So we, as theorists, are never disentangled from our theorizing. Dario Melossi suggests that "it is impossible to claim anything about crime, without spelling out the specific social position one is speaking from" (1994:203). The current dilemmas, contradictions and crucial theoretical pitfalls of contemporary criminology are linked to criminologists not admitting their diversity – in terms of gender, politics, class, race, ethnicity, sexuality and so forth. As a feminist who theorizes as a criminologist, I try to better the position of women – all women – in the course of my work.

As the challenge of, and challenging, feminist criminologies I wish to concentrate on three dominant themes within feminist criminological perspectives which reflect wider debates within feminist research, practice and theorizing:

- the same/difference debates which take intersections of systems of gender, power and dominance seriously;
- vexing questions about powerlessness/victimization and agency;
- debates about feminist standpoints and methodologies, which direct how we ask questions of criminology as feminists.

The same/difference debate
James Messerschmidt pleads:

In order to comprehend what it is about men as men and boys as boys that impels them to commit more crime and more serious types of crime than women and girls – as well as different types and amounts among themselves – we need first a theoretical grasp of social structure and gendered power (1993:29).

A challenge to feminist criminologists (female or male) is to unpick the supposedly natural involvement of men in crime and criminality, and by extension, the unnaturalness of women's involvement. This issue has been extensively debated within feminist criminology (see in particular Heidensohn 1985; Naffine 1987; Daly 1994). My own theoretical preference is to explore how gendered structure contributes to the accomplishment of gender (Messerschmidt 1993; Simpson and Elis 1995). But one version of the debate about same/difference continues to rage in discussions about women's participation in violence, male victims of domestic violence (however small in number this may be), and the gendered dynamics of criminal justice workplaces, such as within policing or the law. It goes as follows: if women can be violent, if men can be victims of domestic violence, and if women can sexually harass or take jobs along side of men, then gender is no longer salient in understanding how violence "works" as a strategy of domination and intimidation. This type of retort also obscures the multiple features of women's and men's everyday lives as we try to manoeuvre around such systems.

Thus, the most compelling challenge is how to widen the discussion about male/female and crime/victimization through the intersections of systems of oppression: gender/race/class/sexualities/disability and so forth. Once again, my personal choice is to explore how individuals – *situationally located* – come to manage and to accomplish these multiple structures which both hinder and assist us throughout our lives. There will always be tensions here. For instance, how does our writing silence the experience of others? After all, when I became concerned about women's experiences of men's violence, I too fought to include women's voices in definitions of violence and abuse. But to what extent do "women's voices" as a category exclude those of black women, poor women, immigrant women and so forth (Crenshaw 1994; Collins 1991; Williams 1991)? Does the emphasis on women's experiences of violence push the focus away from men's experiences of violence (mostly, by the way, at the hands of other men)?

The need to foreground women's experiences (of prison, of violence, of state control, of policing, of risk) should never preclude us asking similar questions of men, a point Gelsthorpe and Morris made in 1988. How such academic theorizing is presented in such a way that does not obscure alternative viewpoints is one of the most challenging features facing today's criminologists. Nelken's (1994) recent edited collection of essays provides some useful insights for taking criminology in a more reflexive direction.

Powerlessness/agency: do we have to choose?

Feminist critiques of criminology are now being themselves criticized for the ways they portray women and men through imagery, as I described recently,

> which persists in contradictory portrayals of women, whether as crime victims of offenders, as heartless, helpless, hopeless, and/or in need of protection or isolation by the father-state, and of men, as altruistic protectors of women, savage violators, or themselves untouched by violence (Nelken 1994:93).

In order to confront the insidious portrayal of women as blameworthy for the violence of men – women asked for it, were masochistic, or took avoidable risks – much of the work exploring the victimization of women emphasized the impact of gendered oppression as a significant contributor to women's subordination.

At the same time, women's offending was explored for its active agency – as a way, perhaps, of celebrating women as independent of men. Many women who committed crime chose to do so, but within a number of constraints (Carlen 1992). The dilemma for theorists, however, is to reconcile the notion of agency with the dynamics of structured oppressions. Why is it so difficult for us in criminology to accept that women and men can be both victims and offenders? To what extent does the experience of victimization effect that of offending, and vice versa? What are the overlaps, and where does offending/victimization not overlap? To me, these questions are some interesting, complex, demanding and creative theorizing in criminology, and could offer crucial information to our praxis in working with both victims and offenders. While I shall not extend this discussion here, it is critical, in combining the theoretical contributions of structural theorists, ethnomethodologists, reflexive criminologists (e.g. Nelken 1994) and standpoint feminists (e.g. Cain 1990) – to find a way through this impasse. If victimization and offending are crucially affected by gender as a dynamic accomplishment, then we must explore how these dynamics – of risk, of avoidance skills, of abusing and using power – can participate in minimizing the individualization of harm. Of course, we are gendered in a deeply embedded cultural context.

Illuminations: feminist standpoints and methodologies

Clearly a significant contribution of discussions and debates about *feminist* methodology and feminist *methodologies* is that the researcher located herself as an active agent in the collection, analysis and presentation of her work. Is there anything to be said for adopting a *feminist perspective* in theorizing in crime and criminology? I think so.

Too often, we assume that theorizing is an impersonal, detached process (as examples of exceptions, see Gelsthorpe and Morris 1990; Nelken 1994). One thing that feminist researchers may agree on (if there is something on which we all could agree! – I can hear the gnarling of critiques now) is that who we are as researchers and as theorists makes a difference to our thinking. This of course means that if we believe that academic work can affect our thinking, and hopefully the practice of so-called justice, our theorizing is as much a product of who we are individually (and collectively) as theorists and researchers. I do believe that my commitment to alleviating the pain violence inflicts drives my work. But it is also driven by an intellectual curiosity, by the entertainment of the ironic twists of crime and criminality, and by the apparently limitless courage and endless creativity of those who confront with instances of crime as routine features of modern life. Illuminating criminology, and the slimy trail of unhappiness crime and violence leaves in its wake, is both a personal and professional challenge.

Notes

1 My successful survival of the haze of sexist treatment does not mean that I ignored the men's behaviour. It made me acutely aware that women were rare in criminology. Things are different now – although in senior positions, women are still rare. See also Stanko (1992).
2 Two supportive academic advisors were Lindsey Churchill and Michael Brown, both faculty of the Sociology Department, Graduate School, City University of New York.

3 More recently, Cooney (1994) argues that this observation is as much an observation about the social nature of legal evidence.

4 I was fortunate to be a member of Michael Grade's Working Group on the Fear of Crime, which convened during 1989, and reported to the Home Office Standing Conference on Crime Prevention.

5 Gelsthorpe's and Morris's (1988) Note 16 comment in their discussion of feminism and criminology in Britain still holds true; many criminologists would still consider feminist criminology as marginal to the criminological enterprise.

CHAPTER 4

Translations and refutations: an analysis of changing perspectives in criminology

Frances Heidensohn

Preamble

In this chapter I shall attempt to reconstruct and analyse the history of certain developments in criminology in the twentieth century. I consider these to have been important and influential developments and they involve my own work and that of a range of respected colleagues. Yet it is not easy to give this narrative a title, nor label the developments in a neat, defining way. One such heading might be "feminist criminology", although I and many others should prefer "feminist perspectives in criminology" (Gelsthorpe and Morris 1990; Rafter and Heidensohn 1995). These names can give rise to problems for the approaches and aspects of the criminological enterprise which they affect. Several writers have suggested that such a title is an oxymoron (Stanko, 1993) or that no good scholarly work can proceed under such a superscription (Smart, 1990).

The first issue to be tackled will be that of names and the power of naming, a section I have called *Translations*. While the main focus here is on a particular series of names and recognitions, it will also be related to other, parallel changes in the discourse about crime which make these shifts easier to accomplish and perhaps more acceptable. Such a situated and relational account is not the most familiar one, and has not been easy to reassemble since this is not a linear nor smooth progression.

Next I consider, under *Awakenings*, the results of having a set of concepts which could be applied to crime in a novel way. In the course of this I also consider both the themes and issues drawn into the subject in consequence and the areas where there was most impact. Last, in *From crime to control* I present my own work from 1985–1995, analysing its main topics and conclusions and attempting to assess both its impact and its future.

Translations

The era of the 1960s (really the period from 1963 to 1973, from the sit-ins at Berkeley and the Beatles' first hits to the oil price shock) saw significant shifts in the study of crime. Indeed for part of that period and for some time afterwards, the academic field was redefined, and most crucially, given a new title "the sociology of deviance". Numerous accounts exist of what new deviance theory brought to, and how it changed, old criminology (Cohen, S. 1981, 1985; Downes and Rock 1988, 1992; Hester and Eglin 1992; Sumner 1994). The main features of its impact included the notion of the social construction of crime and such key concepts as labelling and moral panics.

My own education in criminology began in the early 1960s at the London School of Economics. Paul Rock, in exploring the social organization of British criminology, has described a "fortunate generation" who were recruited into the field in the 1960s and 1970s, came to dominate by the 1980s and were still in command in the mid-1990s (Rock 1988; 1994:133). One of the characteristics Rock notes about these cohorts is their original allegiance to deviancy theory and in what they continue to teach, if they are academics. He and I both belong to one of the earlier of these age groups. We were fortunate not only in that new ideas and opportunities opened up to us in the 1960s but also that we were in time to know criminologists of older generations. The first work I published was a survey of recent research undertaken for Herman Mannheim, then still editing the *British Journal of Criminology*.

When I began graduate studies at the School in 1965, my supervisor was first Alan Little, then Terry Morris. Within a couple of years and when I was already a junior lecturer in the sociology department, David Matza came to spend a year's sabbatical with us.

Paul Rock joined the department the year after I did and David Downes was already teaching in the department of social administration. In July 1968 I remember being at the Cambridge Criminology Conference when the idea of the National Deviancy Conference was being discussed – it took place that November.

The purpose of recording these recollections is not to drop names. It is to set out a context and acknowledge a considerable companionship from other criminologists. And yet little that I could see or learn from this world could help me gain insight into the research tasks that I had set myself. My quest had started from fascination with the problems implied by Barbara Wootton in her 1963 Hamlyn lectures "If men behaved like women the courts would be idle and the prisons empty." Why were women so much less likely to commit (recorded) crimes than men? Why had so little and such inappropriate effort been exerted into exploring this question? Were there not important questions about justice, equity and penal policy which should be reconsidered in the light of this?

Despite all the criminological ferment frothing around us, becoming in due course, the substance of deviancy studies, it did not prove possible to address the questions I wished to answer in a satisfactory way. Other feminist writers have described similar situations: Caroline Ramazanoglu (1989) outlined her difficulties in studying women factory workers in the early 1960s. She depicts a somewhat isolated and very stressful situation in which she conducted her project (1989:429–31) since she chose a conventional positivist methodology and male-centred theory which distorted the women's experiences.

Mine was a somewhat different story. Surrounded by new, challenging ideas in the field, participating in some of the events which were to reshape it (Cohen, S. 1981) none of the new approaches offered insight. My first article sets out the issues quite clearly: "The deviance of women is one of the areas of human behaviour most notably ignored in sociological literature" (1968:160). Why was this and what might be done to remedy it? After raising what Daly and Chesney-Lind were later to call the key issues of the gender ratio and the generalizability problem, I concluded that "approaches to female deviance demonstrate their common inadequacy and inappropriateness for the topic" (1968:169).

With the optimism of the young I insisted that,

> what seems to be needed in the study of female deviance is a crash programme of research which telescopes decades of comparable studies of males ... such a suggestion must await further developments in the study of the deviance of women before we have sufficient material to begin to formulate it into fully fledged hypotheses (1968:171–2).

This article contains most of the major concerns of my own later research and that of several other feminists in the field: explaining sex crime differences, relevance for sociology, social policy and masculinity, and the need for ethnographies. The "liberation causes crime" argument is considered (1968:163) as is standpoint-ism and the rationality of female offending. But it is not expressed in terms which would be used today. At best it can be encapsulated by a writer to whom I shall return as "a syntax opulent with tomorrows" (Friel 1981:42).

Two more papers followed (Heidensohn 1969, 1970) on the imprisonment of women and sex differences in crime. However, the empirical studies which I had undertaken of young women in borstals and of a control group of factory workers remained unpublished. Like Ramazanoglou I felt – and was made to feel – guilty about this, but I had found that "at present we barely possess the basic components for an initial analysis of the deviance of women" (1968:170–1). (I have described elsewhere in greater detail the failure of this project, Heidenshon 1994b.) What was missing of course, was the impact of modern feminism. Later this was to bring two key changes to modern scholarship: concepts and culture. The novel *concepts* related to the analysis of gender and enabled us to think about problems in different ways. The *culture* shift was part of a broader one of the "me" generation which encouraged the study and the support of difference and diversity.

The sources of these developments lay in the burgeoning modern North American feminist movement and their European counterparts and interpreters, from Friedan 1965; Millett 1970; Mitchell 1971 and Oakley 1972.

In the work of Dorie Klein (1973) and Carol Smart (1977) these influences are evident and are transformed by them into new directions in criminology. In reading their contributions I had "not quite a sense of discovery – a sense of recognition, of confirmation of something I half knew instinctively ...[not] an awareness of direction being changed but of experience being of a totally different order" (Friel, 1981:40). The sociology of deviance had given scope for questions about marginal issues in crime and deviance to be raised (such as naturism) and for the status of misfit sociology to be enhanced. None of these perspectives aided the study of gender and crime. Only the importation of a new range of ideas from contemporary feminisms did so.

In this section I have quoted twice from the text of Brian Friel's *Translations*. Friel uses the historic episode of the mapping of County Donegal in the north-west of Ireland by the Ordnance Survey in the 1830s to make profound points about the power of naming, the failure of communication and the loss and disorientation caused by both imposed names and the lack of common language and terms. The academic world of social science in the 1960s and 1970s was "another country" but one for which new maps were being drawn. As one of Friel's characters says "you cannot rename a whole country overnight" (1981:36) and in practice the process of discovery and renaming has been slow and partial. It is nevertheless possible to argue that there is now a situation best depicted as a series of awakenings in the world of criminology.

Awakenings

To reduce a large and complex history down to some major – and simple – shifts, I suggest that there are four linked awakenings to focus on: Naming, Discovering, Spreading, Debating.

Naming

A range of concepts, processes and constructs has been named by feminist scholars. This has not been a simple matter of labelling. Stanko, for example, linked together a series of harms to women: rape, domestic violence, sexual harassment and described them as *Intimate Intrusions* (Stanko 1985). This enabled us to see that gender, power and control were relevant to the analysis of both serious assaults and comparatively minor incivilities. In later work she has extended this analysis to the experiences of men of violence and masculinity (Stanko and Hobdell 1993; Stanko 1994).

Discovering

One of the profoundest awakenings has been achieved through changed approaches to doing research. There is a huge literature on this (see Stanley 1990 and Heidensohn 1994a for accounts) and considerable and continuing debate, see issues of *Sociology* (Gelsthorpe 1992; Hammersley 1992; Holmwood 1995; McLennan 1995 and Ramazanoglu 1992). Amongst innumerable innovative examples to be cited are Carlen's studies of women in prison and female offenders (1984, 1985). In these Carlen employs a variety of approaches: interviews, observations and her own analysis in order to produce a very rounded picture of her subjects.

Spreading

We might say that in the late twentieth century the world woke up to feminism and acknowledged its existence. That is too bold a claim (Rock 1994). It is clear however, that there is a high *recognition* factor which has increasingly been attached to feminist issues, even in criminology. While it may have seemed a distracting and un-welcome diversion to many scholars in the field, the debates around the theme of "liberation causes crime" stemming from the work of Adler (1975) and Simon (1975) were amongst the first to engage wider interest (Austin 1981, 1982; Box and Hale 1983; Heidensohn 1985 and Smart 1979) and to achieve recognition.

Debating

Most important of all the contributions brought to criminology by feminists have been a series of challenges and debates which have been stimulated. These have not only enlivened discussions about gender and crime, they have also helped to extend the frontiers of criminology by focusing on victims of crime (Walklate 1989), the gendered nature of much personal violence and the ways in which such issues were traditionally marginalized. There are many other instances, such as new ways of looking at studies of policing (Young 1990; Fielding 1991).

This summary of new insights into the substance of our subject needs to be seen in a particular relationship to the field as a whole. It is very tempting to use a range of geographical metaphors to illustrate these histories. This was new territory, virgin land. Some of these developments connect quite clearly to mainstream currents of their time. New epistemologies share common origins in the upheavals in social science and politics in the 1960s. Yet other areas began and still remain, relatively remote from central concerns, most significantly perhaps, in the core area of criminological theory itself (Heidensohn and Silvestri 1995; South 1996).

I now turn to my own work for the years 1985–1995. It needs to be seen in the context set out above. Certain caveats ought also to be observed. In reading back over a decade's work, it is possible to see a pattern and clear direction which may be misleading. The heading for this section is *From crime to control* to indicate the change in substantive themes and subjects which I made during this period. While I have changed focus in that way, I still work on topics to do with gender and crime and, as I suggest below, do not foresee that this will cease to be an interesting topic for me or others.

From crime to control

As I have already explained, writing about women and crime had proved difficult in the 1960s. Betsy Stanko illustrates in Chapter 3 in this volume how, by the 1970s, while she faced many problems in her own research, she could and did lay claim both to a vocabulary and a territory which she was able to use with great accomplishment to set a new agenda. In Britain, Carol Smart (1977) performed that pioneer role, taking on the tasks I suggested above of naming and dis-covering aspects of female criminality and challenging received criminological wisdom upon it. Unusually, perhaps, she was cautious about the value of highlighting this topic, arguing that it could be harmful.

Women and crime

When I came to write *Women and crime* (1985) in the early 1980s, it was, therefore at a point of resolution. In one sense, I had been preparing for it for 20 years. It looks both back and forward. All the key material that I had been able to find over the previous years was presented along with a sustained attempt to theorize about two issues: the female share of crime and the criminological neglect of female criminality. For the first aspect it is worth noting that no one could or should try and achieve the same task today in a single text. The volume of material is much vaster and more complex, especially methodologically and theoretically.

Having set out the problem of the low level of recorded female crime and also explored the explanations offered for this phenomenon by earlier criminologists, I embarked upon my own attempt at theory. It was not female *criminality*, I argued, that should be analysed, but rather "move away from studying infractions and look at conformity instead because the most striking thing about female behaviour ... is how notably conformist to social mores women are" (1985:11). The explanatory model outlined owed a great deal to the feminist studies of the 1970s – I began by noting women's participation in social control, both in formal and informal agencies and how this gave them stakes in conformity as well as constraining structures. Most constricting of all, however, were the range of pressures in the home, the street, work place and media, as well as the criminal justice system. All these were, I insisted, conducive to the production of conformity in women. Women were particularly distinctive in being the focus of whole variety of influences and industries targeted not only at their public behaviour but also at their private regulation as wives and mothers. These ideas share features with those of Hirschi and, more particularly, Hagan, who has also addressed gender differences. Hagan has produced several empirical tests of his approach, relating it particularly to family socialization (Hagan et al. 1979). *Women and crime* is, on one level, an interim answer to the conundrums I had faced 20 years before it was published. My debts to feminist analyses are clear and acknowledged in the book. They are, for the most part, not criminological analyses. Instead, I turned to work done on community, the family and welfare systems to supply solutions.

While I tried to give some voice to women offenders themselves in *Women and crime*, drawing on my own previous research and conducting several interviews, the book is essentially an academic exploration. It is a record of an engagement with feminism and something of a disengagement with criminology and the study of deviance. Paradoxically perhaps, its publication into an intellectual climate has changed in some ways since the sixties, and has given me a position from which it is easier to participate in criminological debate.

"Women and Crime: Questions for Criminology" was a significant paper in several ways. Its inclusion in a collection edited by Pat Carlen and Anne Worrall (1987) called *Gender, Crime and Justice* marked in itself a turning point in that such a set of readings could be put together. While I used the opportunity to sum up the story-so-far in characterizing female offenders – noted as economically rational, variously deviant, stigmatised, doubly deviant and doubly dammed – I also tried to assess the impact of feminism on criminology. Had anyone been listening? While an important lesson which should have been noted was the centrality of gender, this did not only mean *women*; I explored several (rather limited) approaches to masculinity and crime. Gaps in research also featured, especially the lack of material on gender and social control.

If there are two poles between which most of my work can be found they are surely housekeeping and adventure. Housekeeping requires central tasks, particularly the ordering and the careful (re)presentation of work, objects and other matters. This can in itself be a radical process, leading to new ways at looking at the familiar or of explaining puzzles. Parts of *Women and crime* and most of the paper in Carlen and Worrall are housekeeping. But some parts of the book are exploratory, seeking new ideas and approaches. As a project, the search for clues to the riddles of female crime and conformity was in itself a major challenge to conventional criminology. A paper which went much further in its radical approach was "Models of justice: Portia or Persephone? Some thoughts on equality, fairness and gender in the field of criminal justice" (1986). In this I was drawing on the stimulating contributions of Carol Gilligan on the "different voice" which women use in various forms of discourse.

While reviewing the literature on gender and justice, I thought that it would be fruitful to write a paper which both summarized this growing body of work and in which I could speculate about equality between women and men in the criminal justice system. This was intended to be a challenging piece, both in the way I was trying to extend the boundaries of the subject and by the language and form used. In the article I questioned the meaning of "equality" in judicial systems for women and men. The conceptual framework I drew on was taken from Carol Gilligan's fascinating work on the "different voice" used by men and women in their analysis of rational behaviour. Gilligan is a psychologist; her approach is based on studies of individuals and does not consider as a sociologist would, historical aspects or social structures. Nevertheless, Gilligan's arguments were stimulating enough to apply to a dual ideal – typical model of justice systems, which I called "Portia" and "Persephone". Gilligan insists that there is evidence of gender differences in justifying behaviour and moral choices; she attributes these to distinctive patterns of socialization. Adult women will be more likely to emphasize *relational* aspects of rationality, while men will focus on *objectivity* and *independence*, because women through their experiences of childbearing and rearing and roles as carers do not value independence as much as men do (Gilligan 1982).

While Gilligan's ideas were the source for part of the argument in "Models of justice", I did not conclude by agreeing that a separate, relationally-based system for women would be desirable. Historical examples (see Rafter 1985) showed that when this form of separate treatment was accorded to women it might be benevolent, but it could also be intrusive and excessive. Daly certainly took up the challenge and responded thoughtfully and critically to it (1989) as well as going on to conduct important work of her own which explored issues of gender differences in punishment (Daly 1994). Tamar Pitch has also reflected this debate in her own work on the significant contributions made by feminist campaigners to discussions on crime and justice in Italy (1990 and 1995).

There are now many more writers contributing to discussions on these and related themes in the ever expanding field of socio–legal studies. Carol Smart, in particular, has deliberately moved the focus of her own work away from criminology (1990) to the sociology of control and regulation.

Crime and society 1989

At the end of the 1980s there were a considerable number of feminist scholars writing about crime and criminology. It was possible at last to have a dialogue about gender and crime. In 1987 the Division on Women and Crime of the American Society of Criminology was founded and in 1988 Daly and Chesney-Lind published a state of the art article, "Feminism and Criminology", which covered US and international developments; the same year saw the publication of a survey of the same topic in Britain by Gelsthorpe and Morris (1988).

These reviews had two themes in common. They noted the rise, vigour and importance of feminist perspectives and at the same time, their relative lack of impact in the mainstream of the subject. Having made the same point in the "Questions for criminology" chapter cited above, I had decided to use the opportunity offered by preparing a criminology text which would not marginalize gender issues nor feminist perspectives.

Crime and society (1989) is a book which presents the heritage of sociological criminology in ways which students, I trust, find accessible and was amongst the earliest texts to include material on gender and crime as central to it. As far as the main themes of this book are concerned, two things are important about *Crime and society*. First, we are all heirs of the major traditions in our discipline; it is what we do with our inheritance that counts. A key feature of the book is that of treasure, of valuing what is passed on, criticizing and using it, discarding only the dross. Second, I tried particularly a focus on the "new" criminological agenda which I thought would dominate the 1990s (the book was written during 1987) – gender crime, victims, fear of crime and policing – and link to the core traditions.

The final chapter contains what for me still remains the right approach to the relationship between criminology and the rest of sociology and social theory, expressed as an analogy:

> The coasts of Britain used to be dotted with tide mills. These mills gained the power to turn their wheels from the water flooded into their mill pools at high tide. Criminology in Britain has functioned rather like a tide mill. The source of its power – the accumulated wisdom and concepts – came from outside … the tides surging and ebbing through sociology (1989:186).

From this, and from other work to be discussed later, it should be clear that while I had searched in earlier work for new terms and concepts with which to address criminological questions, having found a serviceable set of these, I sought to share them. My work thus differs in important ways from some of my colleagues who otherwise adopt similar feminist perspectives. For example, I remained interested in offending behaviour and did not move into the area of victim studies (although I explored certain aspects of these, see Heidensohn 1985 and 1991). Carol Smart (1990) classified my work as "feminist empiricism" in an analysis in which she challenged the notion of "feminist criminology" and where she herself advocates the possibilities of post-modern feminism. In later work I have addressed some of these themes, but remain agnostic if not sceptical about their value.

Crime in Europe

Crime in Europe, which I edited with Martin Farrell, then director of the Institute for the Study and Treatment of Delinquency, was based on some of the papers given at a conference on the subject organized by ISTD in 1988 (Heidenshon and Farrell 1991). The conference was among the first of its kind and the subsequent book was also pathbreaking, a situation which has since altered dramatically (see Heidensohn 1997 for a review of major developments). What was significant about the (highly enjoyable) preparation for *Crime in Europe* for the rest of my work was that it gave me an apprenticeship in comparative criminology which proved invaluable for my next research project on which I had already begun.

Women in control?

When searching for material for *Women and crime* (1985), I had found very little on the topic of gender and policing. In that study I had explored in some depth questions about the role women (and men) play in social control. These questions seemed to me important and interesting and I conceived the idea of a project which would be empirically-based and also have an international comparative framework. The work I had done on policing for *Crime and society* had also drawn me into both discussions about the nature of social control as well as debates about the history and origins of policing. Once again I had observed a gender gap; the literature on the Anglo–American model of policing ignored the distinctive entry of women into both systems. Yet this was not my only nor main motivation. Originally I planned a larger study than I was able eventually to accomplish. My initial aim was to interview women police officers in Britain, the USA and Israel, as well as female security guards and members of similar occupations in those countries, and social workers, nurses and other professionals engaged in what could be termed "control" activities. These ideas were far too ambitious and in the end I settled for a study of 50 officers in Britain and the US. (I also interviewed three British security guards, see Heidensohn 1992.)

Women in control? draws on several strands of social theory; the sociology of social control and of policing, occupational sociology and, for the framework I used in the analysis of police officers' careers, the sociology of deviance. These are all mainstream sources, and deliberately chosen because of this. Women in law enforcement were a minority, and often seen as an anomaly. They have to be placed in their historical and professional context.

Although these sources had, for the most part, glossed over the role played by females in law enforcement, this was not wholly so. Indeed, by the late eighties, it was possible to identify a series of sub genres of writing on policewomen on their integration, on attitudes of male officers to them, and a few feminist analyses, such as the pioneering work of S.E. Martin in the USA (1979) and Jones (1986) in Britain. What had never been done before was to draw all these together and weave them into a broader tapestry.

At one level, there are certain parallels between *Women and crime* (1985) and *Women in control?* (1992). They both take women in minority, deviant positions as their theme. Both present challenges to conventional authorities and their wisdom. But they are otherwise very distinctive. With *Women in control?* I found it possible to write in a series of languages and contexts which could be made mutually comprehensible and compatible. Indeed, other writers had already done some of this work. Thus questions about equality and policing had already been widely discussed. Even greater was the range of work on the nature of policing as a task. In *Women in control?* the two are married up in order to explore fundamental questions about effectiveness and appropriateness in enforcing law and order (Heidensohn 1991:226 ff.). While in the earlier project I needed to find explanatory tools from outside the discipline, this time, "Concepts had to be remodelled on a trial basis. There were plenty to choose from …[although] …it was necessary to rely on 'grounded concepts' derived from the research study itself." (op. cit.: 228).

At the end of the study I found it possible to relate my own conclusions to two sets of theories to which I had referred throughout it. Variations of the "dispersal of discipline" thesis found in the work of Foucault (1977) and Stan Cohen (1985) were insufficient to the "historical complexity and present day com-promises" which my research had revealed. For concepts which did assist such an analysis, I used the work of Connell (1987) who proposed the notions of dominant and subordinate masculinities and related these particularly to "institutionalized violence" (1987: 109). Connell does not provide a fully-worked through explanation about gender and control either, but the most crucial aspects of his work are that he places gender at the core and that he takes masculinity as a problem rather than for granted.

In concluding *Women in control?* I also engaged with debates about the gendered nature of social control to which several feminist authors had contributed. Simple patriarchal explanations did not address the issues which research had raised. There were some parallels in my findings to those of other researchers such as Jones (1986) but what was striking was the much greater focus in feminist work on women as oppressed rather than their participation in forms of control.

Women in control? (Heidensohn 1992) was completed in 1991; in that year an important conference was held in Mont Gabriel in Canada which marked a turning point in my own work and that of other scholars. Three women had met at the 1988 International Society of Criminology Conference in Hamburg and planned a congress which would bring together a world-wide group of those interested in crime and social control from feminist perspectives. Marie Andrée Bertrand from Montreal, Dorie Klein and Kathy Daly from the USA succeeded in their aims and in July 1991 60 of us assembled to discuss topics on women, law and social control. The discussions in themselves were highly stimulating, but what was most significant about this meeting was the opportunity it gave to form links and networks and to open up wider dialogues (Bertrand, Daly, Klein (eds) 1992).

One of the main foci at Mont Gabriel was on how research is to be conducted and how then used: a considerable tension, not exclusive to such gatherings, emerged around these topics. Once more it was the epistemological flows from feminist work outside criminology which were the source for these approaches (Bertrand 1992; Smart 1990; Cain 1991). While I find much of this discussion interesting and potentially important, I do envisage problems with it. At a simplistic level, for instance, the notion of standpoint epistemology (Harding 1981; Smart 1990) can have the effect of narrowing the scope of research in ways which I do not find acceptable. In a paper which I wrote after Mont Gabriel for another seminar in Canada, I analysed some of the contradictions in this approach and illustrated these from my own empirical work (Heidensohn 1994a). Much of this work is complex, sophisticated and not always easy to read. Nor am I sure that it is travelling in any clear direction. It is ironic that, having set out in need of a new vocabulary and having found an appropriate and applicable one, one can find oneself in need of new guides.

In this chapter I have discussed the development of my own criminological work, emphasizing the central roles of gender and feminisms to it. But it is criminology which has remained the main theme; I have tried to improve and enliven it with these distinctive approaches. I have not discussed the activist aspects of all this, partly because they are less relevant here and also, in my case, unlike many of my much more valiant colleagues, these have been mostly with professionals and agencies. My purposes have always been primarily intellectual; the questions I have raised and explored are truly academic. Some of them have come to have policy relevance or to relate to real life concerns and campaigns. In several cases this was serendipitous.

Further futures?

One of the puzzles of academic life is that as one ages, one is regularly asked to predict the future developments of one's own discipline even though one is increasingly less likely to be part of these. I pointed out in one such British Criminology Conference plenary session that we three contributors formed a kind of criminological Jurassic Park. Temptation is, notwithstanding this, all too strong for any social scientist to make such predictions if only since she or he may hope to achieve a Popperian self-fulfilling prophecy. To such temptations I am certainly not immune. I offer two forms of prediction, both based on already known and observable phenomenon. The first concerns the robustness of feminist perspectives, and their wider impact. These will, I think, continue for some years to come, not least because of their wide dispersal in the English-speaking world and their salience for other developments. Yet they will undergo considerable changes, chief of these being massive processes of deconstruction. Thus, central categories of *woman* and of *gender* can no longer be sustained; all is, and must be recognized as difference and division.

What may survive as a legacy are perhaps feminist *approaches* to research (Stanley 1990) which are such good practice that they should be copied as should the stress on gender which has now, finally, been extended to masculinity and crime (Messerschmidt 1993, 1995; Newburn and Stanko 1994). Real prediction can however, be based either only on visions or on current observations extrapolated into future trends. I suggest selecting four broad trends: internationalization, security, reflection and generation gap. I predict that all of these will impact on criminology to some degree and expect them to have an effect on my own work as well as that of others.

Internationalization

Giddens and other sociologists talk of "globalization" and the changes this brings to society. For the criminologist, his or her subject matter is altered as, for instance, international crime and its regulation grows (Levi 1993; Heidensohn 1997). Further, the concepts and understanding of our subject alter as we make more cross-country and cross-cultural comparisons (Rafter and Heidensohn 1995). How far can one apply Braithwaite's notions of integrative shaming, for example, to Bosnia or to Northern Ireland?

Security

For some time, the gaze of policy-makers and analysts alike has extended to embrace offenders and victims, crime and fear of crime, serious offences and civic incivilities. In consequence the subject matter has become security and insecurity and this is also reflected in criminological work, which focuses on victims and their experiences. Wiles and Bottoms (1995) have speculated in a somewhat dystopian way what the future might be like in a security – preoccupied world and I have explored similar issues. Other approaches may include criminal justice audits (Shapland et al. 1995) of local expenditure in order to assess totals and value for money, possibly even the introduction of purchaser/provider divisions.

Reflection

Perhaps it is because the twentieth century is drawing to its close, but the criminology profession is increasingly self-reflective. Thus Nelken (1995) has explored the subject with a view to stimulating it and to achieving the integration of key influences and the penetration of such influences throughout the subject. Others have also considered the nature of influence in the subject (Cohn and Farrington 1994; Levi 1995) and its likely development (South 1996).

The generation gap

No one has yet taken a comprehensive census of criminologists, but there are several examples of surveys of the profession (Rock 1988, 1994; Bertrand 1994). One of the features these show for Britain is that there is a marked demographic deficit between what Paul Rock has called the fortunate generation, now in mid-career, who dominate the field and their successors, who are scarcer and are not, on the whole, in secure academic posts. Marisa Silvestri and I (1995) have already suggested that a key role is played in the discipline by its evangelists, those who write its history since they determine the tradition and its interpretation.

The criminological world predicated on these trends will be a mature one. The world, or those sections of it described as "developed", will form its subject matter. There will thus be more *comparative* work and a need for concepts and theories which provide frameworks for such analyses. Once again, these will have to be borrowed from, for instance, comparative studies of social policy.

Themes and issues for study will, I suggest, be especially concerned with notions of *security* at individual, community and corporate level. Assessment of risk and vulnerability, policies for its reduction, and understanding of personal strategies will become significant. Varied and numerous borrowings from statistics and economics as well as micro-sociological studies will be required. A thoughtful profession will have to prepare either for its demise in the twenty-first century or, in Britain at least, the succession of a much younger generation schooled in a very different fashion.

At the beginning of this chapter I suggested that in my own work the idea of translations had been key. Friel's play, *Translations,* provided a telling source of quotations because he expanded the notion of changing names in a landscape to much broader notions of language, politics and the power of naming. Perhaps the key figure in the play is Sarah, who scarcely speaks, her tongue muted by a speech defect and by fear. The careful teaching given to Sarah gives her some brief voice, but at the end of the play she is mute once more. In all my work I have tried to convey and, at the same time, question experiences. This is part of a process of renewal and expansion. Much of what I have had to say has been about gender and especially the experiences of women in society, but this has not been about a completely separate enterprise from the rest of the subject. Criminology has to keep on renewing itself from outside sources. Having helped to bring in what were once new sources, I hope that their power will be revitalizing in the future.

CHAPTER 5

Copping a plea

Robert Reiner

Discourse on method

I imagine all the contributors to this volume share my quandary of knowing exactly the level of intimacy and revelation appropriate for an intellectual autobiography. When I was studying O-level physics 30 something years ago we were told to write up our experiments to the formula "ADAM was a Roman Catholic" i.e., aims, diagram, apparatus, methods, results, conclusion. ESRC and other grant applications (and to a slightly lesser extent reports of the resulting research), presuppose the same sort of pure rationalistic progress from aims and objectives to results and implications. Yet we know that even in the supposedly harder realms of physical science researchers' efforts are fuelled more by passionate lusts, rivalries and prejudices than by disinterested observation, measurement and deduction (Watson 1968) – with stronger reason presumably in the social sciences, perhaps especially criminology, where the venal side of human practices falls directly under the microscope.

So how far should intellectual autobiography go into the personal undergrowth? Clearly it involves something franker and deeper than the rationalistic fantasies of grant applications and refereed journal papers. But should it cast terror into the assorted cast of partners, paramours, progeny, parents and peers who lurk in the acknowledgements pages of most academic books?

Presumably each contributor will resolve this issue in his or her own way. As I reflected upon my own academic development I came to realize that it had always been motivated at arms' length by factors stemming from my personal biography which are scarcely reflected on the surface of my work. However, these concerns are largely of an intellectual and ethical kind although they are nonetheless by-products of my personal history and circumstances. A psychoanalyst might deem this to be deep denial, but the background to my work is far from the stuff of *News of the World* front pages. This account of the theoretical, political and moral concerns which have animated my research and academic career will not contain any sensational exposés or revelations. But if it is to be honest, it will have to stray beyond the rational and cognitive into some more personal matters.

Breaking into police research: a brief crook's tour

Most of my research and publishing has been on the police. They were the focus of my PhD on police unionism (Reiner 1978b), my text on the politics of the police (Reiner 1985, 1992a), my joint research with Rod Morgan and Ian McKenzie on custody officers (Morgan, McKenzie and Reiner 1990), my book on chief constables (Reiner 1991), several articles on police films (Reiner 1978c, 1981, 1995a), my inaugural lecture on policing a post-modern society (Reiner 1992b), and my joint volume with Sarah Spencer on police accountability (Reiner and Spencer 1993). The main exceptions to this concentration on police research have been a chapter on the Durkheimian tradition in the study of crime and law (Reiner 1984), a couple of literature reviews of the research on race and criminal justice (Reiner 1989a, 1993), a chapter on crime statistics (Reiner 1996a), some papers on recent crime and criminal justice trends (Reiner and Cross 1991; Reiner 1996b), *The Oxford handbook of criminology* which I edited with Mike Maguire and Rod Morgan (Maguire et al. 1994), and the research project I am currently embarked upon with Sonia Livingstone and Jessica Allen on media images of crime since the Second World War (Reiner 1996c).

Apart from the current research on changing media images and the papers on crime trends, most of my work has been in response to outside opportunities and pressures, rather than directly a reflection of my own intellectual or wider concerns. This is especially true of my police research. I am pleased when many police officers I meet assume that I must have some sort of personal or family connection with the police to explain why they have become my specialism, as this implies to me that my accounts of police work and culture have some sense of authenticity. The truth is, however, that I do not have even the most remote personal background or involvement in policing. As far as I can remember the first time I met or spoke to a police officer was when I was interviewing for my PhD. Before that I had never had the occasion even to ask a policeman the time.

I stumbled into police research through a mixture of cowardice, compulsion and convenience. I graduated in economics from Cambridge in 1967. I had started in economics with a genuine passion to understand the sources of poverty and inequality, set the world to rights, and – if possible – earn a living too. At that time the Cambridge economics degree contained the option of doing a large proportion of politics and sociology courses within it. Originally my ambition was to be a mathematical economist, finding a rational solution to the problems of the universe, or at any rate its material ones. Unfortunately, although I had coped well enough with maths at school up to A-level, I was completely thrown by the maths course I followed in the second year at Cambridge.

By the Easter vacation of the second year I realized I was completely out of my depth and heading for disaster at the end of year maths exam. Many of my friends were enthralled by the sociology course then taught primarily by David Lockwood and John Goldthorpe. So as an insurance policy I decided to enter for the sociology option as well. My college arranged a crash course of tutorials with Lee Davidoff, David Lockwood's wife. I remember doing my first essay on Merton's theory of anomie, and being completely captivated by the study of deviance. My conversion was confirmed by the exam results. After a year of maths I only managed to get a third, but my few weeks of enthusiastic reading of a handful of sociology texts netted me a 2.1.

During my third year I concentrated on sociology and politics options, and went on to do the MSc in sociology at the London School of Economics in 1968. By this time my central interest in sociology (apart from theory, everyone's first love) was criminology, and this was heightened by the excellent option on deviance which was taught in inspiring fashion by Terence Morris. In 1969 I was offered a lectureship at the sociology department at Bristol which had recently been formed by Professor Michael Banton. It was understood that I would specialize in teaching deviance, and embark on a PhD on something in that broad area under Michael Banton's supervision. I had the summer vacation to find the precise topic.

If you want a PhD, ask a policeman

It was a sign of both my profound ignorance of the police, and of the neglect of policing within the broader study of deviance at that time, that I did not know that Michael Banton was *the* pioneer of research on the police in the UK and the US. I was not aware that he had published the first sociological book on policing, his classic *The policeman in the community* (1964), although I was familiar with his work on roles and on race relations.

During the summer vacation in 1969 I agonized over a subject for my PhD. In truth the problem was that as a stereotypically repressed grammar schoolboy with an ultra-orthodox Jewish upbringing I had been fascinated to read the appreciative, tell-it-like-it-is studies of "nuts, sluts and perverts" within the burgeoning labelling and naturalistic approaches to deviance. I was drawn to lowlife literature like a shabby Gannex raincoat wearer to Soho. But voyeuristic thrills in the sheltered environs of the university library were one thing, observational field research quite another. I realized with increasing trepidation that immersing myself in the front-line reality of deviant subcultures could be a more fraught and hazardous enterprise than I had bargained for, these anxieties seemed vindicated recently when I read about Dick Hobbs' plucky ventures into the world of career crime in his *Bad business* (1996).

A chance encounter in the library with Jerome Skolnick's riveting seminal study of policing in California *Justice without trial* (1966) seemed to offer an inspired way out. Why not suggest studying what I still, perhaps naïvely, thought of as the right side of the law? When I met him for my first supervision in the autumn of 1969 I tentatively suggested to Michael Banton that I would like to do some research on the police. His eyes lit up as if a starry hand had landed on him from the skies announcing that he had won a triple rollover jackpot. He pulled from his drawer a long list of possible PhD projects which he had put aside for just such an occasion as this. "How about doing a study of the Police Federation?", he suggested. I did not dare confess that I had never heard of the Police Federation, which had not yet become the high profile scourge of Home Secretaries, actual and shadow, that it now is. "Sounds interesting", I mumbled. "I'll think about it."

A couple of days later some assiduous research had resulted in my discovery that the Police Federation was a kind of copper's trade union with a vasectomy; it had all the equipment apart from the power to strike. I was far from clear that I wanted to spend three or more years studying it. However the die had been cast. The next day I was swimming in the deep end of the university pool when a figure shot up from below. It was Professor Banton. "How's your thesis on the Police Federation coming along?", he asked before speeding off again. So there it was.

But what angle was I to take on the Police Federation? I quickly concluded that the straightforward approach, a historical account of its structure and functioning, had already been accomplished more or less definitively by Tony Judge, the editor of *Police* (the Federation's monthly magazine), in a couple of his books (Judge 1968; Reynolds and Judge 1968. These have been updated by Judge 1994).

So like most PhD students I fell back on the safety of intellectual pastiche. As I mentioned earlier my first sociology lecturers had been David Lockwood and John Goldthorpe, and the latter had been my supervisor during my final undergraduate year. I was steeped in their classic studies of trade union and class consciousness, *The blackcoated worker* (Lockwood 1958) and *The affluent worker* trilogy (Goldthorpe et al. 1968, 1969). Why not try and adopt a similar approach to the career, work situation, and socio-political perspective of police officers, who were workers after all, albeit of a highly distinctive kind? The idea had several appealing aspects to me. I could follow the methodological models of some of the most influential empirical studies in British sociology at that time. I could combine the two main ingredients of my formal academic education, economic sociology and the sociology of deviance. Not least, I liked the mild chutzpa of calling the project *The blue-coated worker* (1978b) in honour of these roots.

Instrumental or intrinsic inspiration? confessions of a PhD student

Twenty-plus years later I must confess that my PhD work was conducted largely at intellectual arms' length. It scarcely connected with any of my genuine theoretical, moral or political concerns, and much of my orientation to the work was instrumental rather than intrinsic (to borrow the terminology of the thesis, derived from Lockwood and Goldthorpe). No doubt this is true of many other, perhaps most, PhDs, due to fear and lack of intellectual self-confidence rather than straightforward careerist considerations.

Although my start in police research was serendipity not rational choice, as I will argue later, I subsequently found it a suitable vehicle for exploring issues which I did have an intrinsic concern about. What limited my PhD was not that policing as a topic inherently could not be an expression of genuine theoretical interests but that I was seeking the intellectual security blanket of modelling the research on established paradigms.

Post-doc blues

My continuation in police research after completing and publishing my thesis was once again the product of outside pressures and opportunities, not a truly autonomous choice. By coincidence I finished my PhD, and began publishing papers and subsequently a book based on it, just as the Police Federation, initially about as obscure a topic as one could find, became front page news. Partly this was because they were engaged in a bitter and protracted pay dispute, including threats of police industrial action for the first time in 50 years, which culminated in the Edmund Davies pay review in 1978.

Even more significantly these were the years in which the Police Federation began a high profile and controversial 'law and order' campaign which was a coded "vote for Margaret Thatcher" message in the run-up to 1979 and all that. The Police Federation, once the "toothless tiger" (as it was commonly referred to by my PhD sample of members), had suddenly bit the Labour Government where it hurt (post-election polls in 1979 suggested the law and order campaign had been a significant source of vote switching to the Tories).

For me it was a question of being in the right place at the right time (the favourite explanation of career success in the police force offered by my respondents in my PhD interviews). The advantage of doing an obscure topic for a PhD is that if it ceases to be obscure you are likely to have a monopoly of expertise on it. On the basis of my research I was well placed to comment and publish on the newly prominent pressure group, the Police Federation.

Apart from the politicization of my particular research pet, the Police Federation, the second half of the 1970s also saw policing in general become increasingly central to political conflict. Reflecting this it was during these years that the police began to be studied on a significant scale in British criminology. Soon after I began my PhD Michael Banton initiated a series of three biannual conferences on the sociology of the police at the University of Bristol (for an account of the influence of these see the symposium on Banton's work in *Policing and society* Chatterton 1995; Holdaway 1995; Reiner 1995b).

At that time police research was a small cosy club with hardly a handful of members. Apart from Banton himself there was the PhD and later book by Maureen Cain (Cain 1973), John Lambert's work on police and race relations (Lambert 1970), John Martin and Gail Wilson's study of police manpower (Martin and Wilson 1969), and Maurice Punch's study of public demand for policing (Punch and Naylor 1973). There was also a rapidly growing body of excellent American research, the relevance of which to Britain was much debated (the American giants of police research were producing some of their major works at this time, see Skolnick 1966; Wilson 1968; Bayley and Mendelsohn 1968; Reiss 1971; and slightly later Manning 1977 – which echoed Banton in being based on studies both of American and British policing).

Following in the wake of this early research was a small band of PhD researchers like myself, notably Mike Chatterton and Simon Holdaway. As late as 1979 the extent of police research in this country was still small enough for Simon Holdaway to edit a volume of less than 200 pages which was a definitive sampling of the state of the field at that time (Holdaway 1979). The still continuing explosion of British police research only began in the early 1980s, in the wake of the Thatcherite politicization of law and order (I have examined this growth in detail in Reiner 1989b, 1992c, 1994).

My first publication after my PhD was an article summarizing it which I sent to *New Society*: "Reds in blue?" (Reiner 1976). This proved to be fruitful in many more ways than being the first notch in a curriculum vitae (apart from a paper on the sociology of country and western music which *The New Edinburgh Review* had published in 1973). Paul Barker the editor of *New Society* had a remarkable eye for spotting trends before they emerged. Once I had become known to him he kept commissioning me to write articles on aspects of policing which were about to hit the headlines. This led me to write a series of articles on different aspects of policing just as they became controversial, and eventually meant I had covered the whole field in embryo. These articles in effect became the basis for the general book on policing which I wrote in the appropriate Orwellian year, 1984, *The politics of the police* (Reiner 1985, 1992a).

I was particularly pleased with Paul Barker's anticipation of the issue of the militarization of public order policing after the Lewisham and other clashes at National Front rallies in 1977–8. He commissioned me to write an article on police public order tactics in 1979 which I spent several weeks researching. Unfortunately, he then shelved it and as the months went by I grew resigned to the fact that it would probably never be published. My frustration was consoled by an especially large royalty cheque (conscience money from him?), and the fact that I could tell dinner parties that I had earned more from one unpublished article than all my published work put together. In early April 1980 I flew to Los Angeles for a six- month sabbatical. The next day the first of the 1980s urban riots erupted in St Paul's, Bristol, within earshot of my house. I was recovering from jet lag when my father rang me from London, to congratulate me on being prophetically able to write about a riot which was taking place while I was flying across the Atlantic. I subsequently discovered that *New Society* had dusted off my old public order policing article and published it with a headline and introductory sentence to make it appear as if it was an instant comment on St Paul's (Reiner 1980).

No enemies to the left

The period in the late 1970s, during which I was producing these papers on different aspects of the growing political debate on policing, was one in which the intellectual centre of gravity in British sociology was very heavily Marxist. The dragon of left idealism had not as yet even been named, let alone slain, by St Jock and the new left realists. It permeated much of deviance theory as a taken-for-granted, scarcely articulated set of attitudes, as its counterparts did in other areas of sociology. Just as the prospect of change in a socialist direction departed from the tent of political reality into an Arctic darkness, to be gone for a very long time, academic sociology and criminology were churning out papers, debates and "interventions" galore which made sense only if the Marxist millennium was around the next corner.

This climate was reflected in my main publications in the late 1970s (especially Reiner 1978d and e), which were probably the first academic papers on policing written from an explicit Marxist perspective (apart from the contemporary work of Cyril Robinson in the USA such as Robinson 1978). These were uncharacteristic for me, in terms of my overall life and experience. Although (because?) I come from an overwhelmingly c/Conservative family background I cannot ever remember not being somehow radical in my political beliefs and commitments. I had no enemies to the left, and an implacable moral and intellectual hostility to the right, but a perhaps even more firmly rooted aspect of my outlook and personality has always been a deep pessimism about the prospects of anything other than piecemeal progress and a scepticism about utopian enthusiasms. For reasons of personal biography which I will sketch later, I am a dyed-in-the-wool emotional Menshevik, with a perennial soft-spot for heroes destined for the dustbin of history.

Nonetheless, when a former University of Bristol colleague who had moved to become editor of *Marxism Today*, Martin Jacques, commissioned me in 1977 to write an analysis of recent developments in policing for his journal, I leapt at the chance for a number of reasons. I must confess to a frisson of childish glee at the opportunity to shake up my bourgeois parents. More seriously I was already somewhat vexed about the root and branch hostility towards the police then dominant on the Left. It gave me a chance to develop my own more ambivalent analysis of the police as a "contradictory class location", in E.O.Wright's terminology which was then being busily debated in the pages of *New Left Review* (Wright 1976).

My feelings on reviewing my *Marxism Today* article and other papers I wrote in that mould are as ambivalent and contradictory as the class location I attributed to the police. On the one hand I remain pleased with my critique of the vulgarization of Stan Cohen's concept of moral panic (Cohen 1972) which then prevailed in radical criminology. The dominant left criminological cliché was that crime was a phenomenon of tabloid headlines rather than the streets, with the function of ideologically legitimating more repressive social control.

I argued instead that crime was a genuine problem, albeit one which could be the basis of disproportionate fears exploited by the right, and that as it particularly blighted the lives of the poorest and most vulnerable sections of society it ought to be taken more seriously by the left. I can still reread my premature left realism with some satisfaction. I also remain happy with the basically structuralist diagnosis and policy recommendations about crime which I offered: that the sources of crime are rooted in wider social arrangements, above all the political economy and culture, so that criminal justice – however efficiently and effectively conducted – is at most marginally important in controlling crime.

What now makes me squirm with embarrassment is the section of my *Marxism Today* paper which attracted the most favourable responses at the time. These are the pages in which I attempted to sketch out the way that the contradictory class location of the police, as simultaneously workers and state agents, could be politically exploited to prise them away from conservatism to support for revolution. To my chagrin I pursued the ultra-utopian hare of speculating on what shape the police would take in a socialist society, no doubt before they withered away altogether. Like the last few pages of Taylor et al.'s 1973 classic text *The new criminology* (then a Bible to me as to so many criminologists of my generation, cf. Rock 1994), these passages now seem to me almost a caricature of what Jock Young has since come to label "left idealism" (Young, J. 1994).

Look for the silver lining

I felt uncomfortable with the rather vulgar Marxist analysis which permeated the papers I wrote in the late 1970s even at the time. But I was emotionally carried along by a desire not to break ranks with the wishful thinking which then dominated so much British left sociology.

What broke this intellectual logjam for me was an experience which at first I found traumatic and struggled against. As a consequence of the 1981 cuts in university finance, the University of Bristol developed a plan which included cutting the sociology department drastically. This was to be achieved as far as possible by redeployment rather than redundancy. The little local difficulty for me in their grand design was the godfather-style "offer" made to me that I might "like" to be redeployed to the law department.

My perception of law at that time (a prejudice which I suspect was shared by most if not all my social science colleagues) was that it was a matter only of learning rules, black-letter in the extreme. I thought of it as vocational rather than intellectual, a bastion of authoritarianism. I resisted leaving the sociology department and what I treasured, at least at the moment it was about to be wrenched away from me, as its commitment to progressive values and theoretical exploration. Nonetheless after the initial kicking and screaming I bowed to the pressures of the university plan, and transferred to the citadel of rational legal authority in the mock-Gothic spire of the Wills Memorial Building.

Looking back I realize that my fears only betrayed my lack of sociological insight. In the event I have now worked in three law departments as a criminologist (Brunel and London School of Economics succeeding Bristol). I have found that if anything the intellectual and political atmosphere of academic law is more liberal and concerned with theoretical rather than merely practical and policy agendas than sociology.

There is a very clear sociological basis for this, had I only thought it through. Apart from the odd social scientist gone astray like myself, academic lawyers have nearly all got far more lucrative career opportunities in practice than the groves of academe. They are a self-selected group of people who have made deliberate choices to forego instrumental rewards for the intellectual and political values in which they are more interested. Concern with theoretical and ethical issues is at least as central to the culture of the academic law departments I have worked in as it is to academic sociology.

For me personally I found the transfer intellectually liberating, once the pains of transition had abated. I was left to my own devices academically so long as I fulfilled the basic remit of continuing to publish something. The hidden agenda was my mere presence as a token sociologist demonstrating the department's concern to move away from its traditional black-letter approach to law towards a more socio–legal, contextual one. This was made clear to me at the farewell party held when I was leaving for Brunel. David Feldman (now professor of public law at Birmingham) gave a valedictory speech. They had wanted me, he said, to import a touch of the modern social world into the fusty corridors dominated by the law reports, and I had succeeded amply, bringing them smack bang up-to-date with the culture of the 1950s.

The politics of the police

From the late 1970s onwards, while still in the sociology department at Bristol, I had been planning to write a general book on the politics of the police. My interest in this grew out of my PhD research which uncovered the increasing role of the Police Federation as a political pressure group, and the series of articles I had been commissioned to write on current policy controversies involving the police by journals like *New Society* and *Marxism Today*. I was much taken also with John Griffith's *The politics of the judiciary* (1977), the first edition of which was then still controversial. At the back of my mind was the dream of achieving a similar exposé of another arm of the state's repressive apparatus.

I was hoping to plug two specific gaps in police literature and debate. Although there was a burgeoning scholarly library on the police, it contained either empirical monographs or interventions on specific policy issues. There was nothing tying together all the research and debates. The policy literature (and to a lesser extent the academic literature) was also very polarized, politically and analytically. The police were either paragons or pigs; defenders of civilization as we know and love it, or the jack-booted repressive arm of the state.

For theoretical and moral/political reasons (both growing out of my personal background as I will show in the concluding section) I was drawn to try and bridge this increasingly gaping chasm. In general political terms I was firmly on the left, and shared the fashionable criticisms then being advanced about many of the actual activities of the police. At the same time I felt that these were partly vitiated by an implied utopian standpoint about what was possible.

To me the police were necessarily dirty workers, in Everett Hughes' phrase (Hughes 1961), doing the tragically inescapable job of managing, often coercively, the symptoms of deeper social conflicts and malaise. They were a necessary evil in any complex society even if this was over-determined at times by a surplus degree of malpractice or repression due to the especially unjust or contradictory character of social structure and culture in particular periods. This sense of the police function as Janus-faced was pithily captured in the title of a paper I later read by Otwin Marenin: the police dealt both with "Parking tickets and class repression" (Marenin 1983). Whereas this was, in the late 1970s, a heretical view on the left, I was encouraged by E.P. Thompson's passionate and wittily eloquent espousal of it (Thompson 1980).

This basically tragic perspective on the police role was the leitmotif of two theoretical analyses of policing which influenced me increasingly in the late 1970s. The image of the good police officer as a tragic hero was elaborated at length in a sensitively observed, Weberian analysis of the police by Ker Muir Jr. (Muir 1977). The inevitably thankless and ultimately Sisyphean character of police work was also implied in Bittner's celebrated theorization of the police as the wielders of the state's monopoly of legitimate force, called upon to intervene in any emergency conflict situation (Bittner 1974). Both accounts were encapsulated in a passage from Weber which ultimately appeared as the frontispiece to *The politics of the police*. "He who lets himself in for politics, that is, for power and force as means, contracts with diabolical powers and for his action it is *not* true that good can follow only from good and evil from evil, but that often the opposite is true. Anyone who fails to see this is, indeed, a political infant." (Weber 1918).

Although the limited sympathy for the police which this tragic perspective implied was heretical on the left in general in those days, I had discovered that it was the normal position for empirical social researchers on the police. This itself was demonstrated by a little-known but fascinating reflexive empirical study by one of the doyens of American criminology, Al Reiss, which gave me the great comfort of showing me that my own reactions to the police were boringly typical (Reiss 1968).

In the mid-1960s Reiss had organized and conducted for the Presidential Commission on Law Enforcement the largest-scale piece of observational research on the police ever carried out. As a sidewind of this he had the great idea of researching the researchers. Dozens of students were recruited to be the observers who rode along with the police for hundreds of hours noting exhaustively their myriad transactions with the public. The views of these student observers on the police were ascertained by Reiss before the research began. These were the standard suspiciousness of the police which was normative for 1960s students. The observers were questioned again after riding with the hated pigs for many hours in the intimacy of squad cars. All the students had modified their views to become more sympathetic to the officers whose tribulations they had observed and come to understand better.

What was particularly fascinating was that this was not a question of simply going native. The students continued to recognize the aspects of policing which had initially made them hostile, such as racism or brutality, and still condemned these. They found ways of reconciling this condemnation of some police actions with their new sympathy for the cops as human beings, applying different perspectives according to the disciplines from which they had been recruited. The law students thought the problem lay in bad laws administered by good cops, the management students attributed the blame to poor management, and so on. What was particularly poignant to me was the stance adopted by the sociology students – the same structuralist perspective as I had espoused. Cops, like the deviants and other clients they encountered, were fundamentally benign human beings, who were sometimes driven or drifted into undesirable behaviour because of the structural pressures of a social system which needed reforming to make it more just. As with so much sociological analysis of one's own situation, what was subjectively experienced as an arduous personal intellectual odyssey turned out for me to be par for the course.

Thus when I wrote *The politics of the police* it was intended to do two things. My primary purpose was to contribute to the enormously impassioned political debates then raging around the police. The book was written during the miners' strike when the political controversies about policing, which had been building up throughout the late 70s and early 80s were at their height (reflecting the general politicization of law and order (Reiner and Cross 1991; Downes and Morgan 1994).

On the one hand the Thatcher government had built the police up as the battering-ram of the strong state which, in Andrew Gamble's phrase (Gamble 1988), was the paradoxical precondition of the free economy at which they aimed. To the Conservatives at that time the police were a beloved pet, the pampered special case exception to their aversion to all things public (especially such expensive ones).

On the other hand a left-wing consensus of hostility to the police had developed. On this view the police were over-mighty oppressors who had grown far too big for their jackboots. Their powers, resources and status all needed cutting down to a smaller size, if not eliminated altogether, by a democratization of the police. The minimum demand was for complete subjection of policing to control by democratically elected local police authorities. Even the Left Realists, the pragmatic pole of left debate on criminal justice, argued for a "minimalist" conception of the police role and powers (Kinsey, Lea and Young 1986).

My practical purpose in writing *The politics of the police* was to intervene in this polarized argument in support of a middle way. This would recognize the inevitable requirement in a complex society for a body capable of regulating emergency conflicts with the use of legitimate force. Policing was both inevitable and inevitably dirty work, exercising power over someone in a conflict. The most that could be accomplished was not the elimination of this necessary evil but its subjection to values decided upon by the democratic process. In the actual context of the mid-80s the police *were* being used to maintain and increase social injustice on behalf of an increasingly privileged minority. But what needed to be done was change society and policing within that, not to alienate the police by regarding them as intrinsic enemies. Although formally my polemic was aimed equally at the left and the government, the greater passion was expended against the former, with whom I identified, than the latter, whom I regarded as irredeemably morally corrupt.

In order to advance my political argument, I reviewed as comprehensively as my knowledge allowed the historical and sociological literature on the police. Thus the book served also as a textbook on policing, the first to be published in this country. The polemical side of the book was quickly rendered redundant by political developments. Once the Conservatives had accomplished the virtual destruction of organized labour, courtesy of the rough policing directed at the miners and print-workers, the police ceased to be vital tools of their overall project. The police rapidly became as redundant as most other traditional workers, at least in the pampered style the Conservatives had hitherto supported. Already by 1988 the government was indicating in unequivocal terms that severe police expenditure cutbacks were imminent. During the 1990s the police/Tory relationship became as cold and icy as any royal romance of the 80s.

On the other hand Labour leaders and shadow Home Secretaries began to woo the spurned police with increasing ardour. They appeared increasingly eager to shed the electorally damaging image of being depicted as anti-police. Neil Kinnock set the tone in 1986 with an interview in *Police Review* in which he confessed that he had always really had the boyhood ambition of being a police officer. Unfortunately, for some inexplicable reason, he had ended up as Leader of the Opposition instead. Since then Tony Blair and now Jack Straw have also gone out of their way to court the cops and establish their credentials as tough men of law and order.

Thus the polemical side of *The politics of the police* was rapidly superseded by events. However, its role as a textbook has survived, and I would be working on the third edition now if I was not writing this chapter. The second (and hopefully the third) editions have lost the political purpose of campaigning for a middle course on policing. This has become the taken-for-granted stance of New Labour, and I almost have a nostalgic longing for the old days of police bashing. What I hope to develop in the third edition is the analysis of the concept of policing, and of the transformations in policing in what may be called a postmodern society, which I began to explore in my inaugural lecture (Reiner 1992b) and my contribution to *The Oxford handbook of criminology* (Reiner 1994). Before these current concerns I did carry out a pet empirical project on chief constables which I shall discuss briefly first.

Top of the cops

Chief constables (1991) was the book of mine which attracted the most attention at the time of its publication, largely because it provided some new empirical material on issues of current controversy. However, for the same reason, it was really a portrait of a significant criminal justice elite at a particular moment of development, albeit a particularly interesting one and its relevance now is largely historical. I studied chief constables at a crucial point of change, when a generation was being replaced by another, and even before the book appeared more than half my subjects had retired. A decade later none are still in the police force (though a few are still in police related occupations like the HM Inspectorate of Constabulary).

The point at which I studied chief constables was when the old post-war styles (which I dubbed *bobbies, barons and bosses*) were being replaced almost wholesale by a new breed which was being cultivated by the Home Office in the Scarman mould, whom I called *bureaucrats*. These were highly educated, politically adroit, human-relations sensitized managers, oriented to the cultivation of consensus, inside and outside their forces. They were sharply con-trasted with either the autocratic disciplinarians or the everyday bobby promoted to top cop of the old school. Sadly the post-Sheehy and Police and Magistrates' Court Act "reforms" are threatening the Scarmanesque diplomatic type of chief constable. Current Home Office pressures are leaning towards a new type: the *businessman*, cynical yuppies who know the performance measures for everything and the meaning of nothing.

To me the most interesting finding of my study was the extent of behind-the-scenes Home Office influence on the chief constables. Some of the revelations made to me in interviews so contradicted official denials of this that I was tempted at times to blow the whistle. One particular afternoon in the spring of 1987, a few days before the General Election, I remember standing on the station platform on my way home after an interview, wrestling with the decision whether to break all my pledges of confidentiality and phone *The Guardian*. I had just been told of direct instructions from Mrs Thatcher during the miners' strike to establish an intelligence unit to cover trade unionists who she was convinced were under Russian influence (Reiner 1991: 191). In the end fear (for myself and my informant) rather than professional ethics persuaded me that no-one would pay any attention anyway, so I took the train – not the risk.

The finding of Home Office domination of key policing decisions was novel at the time, but has since become commonplace. It was replicated by the Policy Studies Institute study of key police decisions in the last few years (Jones, Newburn and Smith 1994). It has in any event become quite explicit in the Police and Magistrates' Court Act 1994 and other parts of the current reform package. Although my research on chief constables was fascinating to carry out and contributed some interesting empirical results, it was not informed by any new theoretical concerns, so I will not dwell on it any further here.

Rosebud

The above account of how I came to do the various projects on policing which have occupied most of my career has emphasized the surface elements of chance and the political concerns which prompted it. For many years I had no answer to my parents' frequently voiced question how on earth had I ended up doing so much work on the police. It just seemed one random opportunity or commission after another. However in recent years I have come to realize that, in the Marxist cliché, it is no accident.

In this concluding section I will try and make explicit the underlying intellectual and moral concerns which have allowed the police to become my anthropological tribe, in terms of which it was possible to explore a host of different theoretical, moral and political issues. The police were especially suitable because (as I have expressed it in several papers in recent years) the police are a kind of social litmus paper. They register all major changes in the broader social structure and culture. This is because the police, as the specialist regulators of social conflict both at an everyday micro level and at a macro political level, face problems which are continuously evolving as sensitive reflections of general social developments.

The police, and more broadly crime and deviance, have been congenial subjects for me because even though they are concretely far removed from my own life experience (other than through research) they have served as coded vehicles of other, more personal concerns. Like "Rosebud", the long discarded childhood sleigh which animates all Orson Welles' adult actions in *Citizen Kane*, my interest in policing, crime and deviance is derived from deeper roots in my personal biography which I will sketch briefly.

I was born in Hungary shortly after the Second World War and came to England as a refugee in 1948. Many years ago a senior Police Federation official thought he saw in this the source of what he perceived as my radicalism on policing. At a police conference (where he had been sampling rather too much of the Bull's Blood and other Hungarian wine on offer) he warned some chief constables not to talk to me as I was a "subversive". He had discovered that I had been born in Hungary and was therefore a "dangerous Red". I asked how he knew I was born in Hungary and he replied that he had seen my Special Branch file. If I have such a file it presumably does record the fact that I was born in Miscolc, Hungary in January 1946. However, the Federation official's deduction from this was precisely the opposite of what I understand as the effects of my origins on my police research.

My parents were both Jewish holocaust survivors, most of whose families had perished at the hands of the Nazis. They left Hungary as refugees shortly after I was born. This was just before the Soviets, who represented to them the threat of another totalitarian regime (albeit of opposite ideological hue and without the same genocidal intent) had cemented their grip. To my parents England, Churchill and all symbols of the British way of life – from roast beef to bobbies – represented salvation.

This made me a classic example of a phenomenon analysed by Perry Anderson in his paper "Components of the national culture" (Anderson 1968). In this he attributes the stubbornly empiricist flavour of British social theory to the enthusiasm for pragmatism and other supposedly British values of the generation of white émigrés who fled totalitarianism in the 30s and 40s. Many such refugees became intellectually dominant in British social thought in the 1950s, for example, Popper and Hayek. With the enthusiasm of converts they hallowed all aspects of British culture and liberal democratic political institutions.

When I read the Anderson paper I recognized this pattern in myself, even though unlike the older generation of white émigrés the experience did not incline me to conservatism. It did however inoculate me against the wilder extremes of police bashing common on the left from the 60s to the 80s. In particular it made me utterly contemptuous of the student radicals' trivialization in calling the British police fascists or SS. I was acutely aware of the potential for abuse which was inextricable from the police role as the repositories of the state's monopoly of legitimate force. But I was also imbued with a deep sense that the British police tradition (and others derived from it) had at least to a large extent succeeded in minimizing the ultimately inescapable dangers. This feeling was common to those with my experience. The title of a recent book collecting a variety of reminiscences of child refugees from Hitler captures the point. It quotes the poignant words of one little girl on seeing a British bobby after years of the SS: *And the policeman smiled* (Turner 1990).

I believe this white émigré psychology underlies my interest in analysing the sources of the British police advantage, which is most explicit in *The politics of the police*. My experience as a child refugee and a member of the second generation, as a child of Holocaust survivors also underlies my affinity for the tragic, Weberian perspective on policing exemplified in the work of Bittner and Ker Muir, and discussed earlier. I have a scepticism of utopianism and concepts like harm reduction and damage limitation are more congenial to me than the pursuit of happiness. I find the negative, Rabbinic version of the Golden Rule formulated by Hillel ("do not do to others what you do not want done to yourself") a preferable and more realizable guide to ethical behaviour than the positive version found in the Pentateuch and the New Testament ("love your neighbour as yourself" cf. Kaufmann 1963 Chap.VIII).

This underlies my position that policing, as the unfortunate necessity of using evil means – violence – to attain good or at least minimize harm, is ultimately inescapable in some situations (a predicament well analysed by Klockars as the "Dirty Harry" problem: Klockars 1980). The only viable political and analytic project is to minimize those situations where violence becomes tragically necessary and to imbue the dispensers of legitimate violence with the means and culture to achieve minimal force interventions. Understanding the structural and cultural conditions of good or bad policing in this sense remains to me a worthwhile and compelling theoretical issue.

My more general interest in understanding trends and patterns in crime, deviance and social control (including criminal justice and policing) derives partly from the same roots of my refugee and survivor experience. But it is more directly a product of my religious education and upbringing. I come from an ultra-Orthodox Jewish family, went to an ultra-Orthodox primary and grammar school (which was also the alma mater of several other academics who work in the criminology/criminal justice field including Professor David Nelken of Macerata University, Professor Gerald Cromer of Bar Ilan University, and Professor Michael Freeman of University College, London), and then for six months (during what is now called my gap year) to a Talmudical college in Gateshead. I grew up in Golders Green in what was (and is) virtually a self-imposed ghetto of the ultra-Orthodox. Until I went to Cambridge at the age of eighteen my only contact with non-Jewish (or even Jewish secular) culture was vicariously through books and the mass media, to which I became addicted from the age of four or five. My only contact with non-Jewish people was fleeting and impersonal – in shops or on public transport.

Despite this I began to question my faith during my A-level studies. This was particularly prompted by learning about the Reformation for A-level history. I identified the Jewish world I had grown up in with medieval Catholicism, and saw all the questions of the Protestant reformers as ones applicable to the Judaism I had been taught and until then absorbed without question. This led on to a project I only abandoned after a few years when it seemed to be an unattainable chimera; trying to read all the classic works of Western, particularly modern, philosophy. I also read my way voraciously through Freud in an effort at self-analysis, and then became more sceptical after encountering the three *pelicans* books by Hans Eysenck which all my contemporary sixth-formers seemed to read: *Sense and nonsense in psychology* and its companion volumes.

This all made me a fanatical, militant atheist and rationalist for many years. My heroes were Freud, Bertrand Russell, John Stuart Mill, Popper and the like. I enjoyed nothing better than going to my religious lessons and using their arguments in fierce contests with my teachers and more devout fellow pupils. However, during my anti-religious teen and early adult years I never lost the personal ethical code I had derived from my upbringing (encapsulated in the negative Golden Rule I quoted earlier: "do not do to others what you do not want done to yourself").

It underlay my early attraction to socialism, and I have never ceased being unable to understand how not just many but most of the religious world who claim to espouse that ethic are conservative. My major argument against the faith of my childhood was (and remains) the Problem of Evil in logical terms. In emotional terms I have never understood how religious people (not just Jewish ones of course) can hold and enforce values (for example, about homo-sexuality, the place of women, ethnic differences, and social and economic policy) which to me seem flagrantly at odds with the Golden Rule which they claim is paramount. To me personally commitment to a socialist and progressive position is an inescapable logical outgrowth of religious ethics, a position I found eloquently expressed for me in Isaac Deutscher's essay "The non-Jewish Jew" (Deutscher 1968).

My attraction to sociology, in particular the sociology of crime and deviance, stemmed from all this. When I first encountered it in the mid to late 60s it was dominated by the arguments about labelling theory. These seemed to speak directly to my predicament as a young man trying (with little success) to liberate myself from guilt about deviating from the practices and beliefs with which I had been raised. More than abstract moral philosophy the debates about what should be criminalized, how social groups defined and applied deviant labels, captured dilemmas with which I was struggling personally. At the time I embraced the fashionably dominant libertarian position on matters I regarded as ones of purely private morality (sexuality, censorship, drugs and the like) while main-taining an absolutist radical stance on questions concerning how people should treat each other and how societies should be organized, including what laws states can and should enforce. Not surprisingly this made me suspicious of the police as the bulwarks of conventional morality and the political status quo. However, as described earlier, I quickly modulated this to a position more sympathetic to their structural predicament, a progression common to most sociological observers of the police.

In my early days at Bristol University, one of my colleagues in the sociology department, Ian Hamnett, passed me a note during a faculty board meeting which has haunted me ever since. I was making some ultra-politically correct point as was then my wont. His note read: "He who marries the Spirit of the Age is quickly divorced." In truth the divorce was already occurring. No sooner had I left the confines of the ghetto and actually entered the world of secular academe (which I had read about in awe for so many years) before I began to experience some disillusion with the latter and increasing interest and sympathy for my roots.

On the one hand I discovered to my disappointment that progressive secular intellectuals in the flesh were far from the selflessly rational, humane and ethical beings conveyed by their books. I had always been mystified by the contrast between the theoretical Golden Rule ethic of Orthodox Judaism and the actual intolerance and lack of humane concern for others which is embodied in their moral and political conservatism. However, by the same token I have never been able to come to terms with the contrast between the egoism and inconsiderate treatment of people in personal relationships which is often accepted behaviour by those who nominally espouse values of radical concern for social justice. On a small-scale this disillusion set in at my very first staff meeting. Thirsting for some debate about intellectual or political matters, I was shocked to find the agenda dominated by heated discussions about car-parking spaces and the allocation of a merit increment.

At the same time, no sooner was I living away from the Jewish world from which I had yearned to liberate myself in my teenage years when I began to pine for at least some aspects of it. In particular I began to read assiduously on contemporary Jewish culture, which my religious education steeped in the study of ancient texts had neglected. I read particularly eagerly studies of the Holocaust – which my parents had until then tried to hide from me. I also read voraciously about the consequent establishment of the state of Israel and the history of Zionism, aspects of contemporary Jewish life which my ultra-Orthodox school had played down because of ambivalence about the secular character of most of the Zionist movement.

For some years I maintained a secular Jewish identity, but gradually experienced some rapprochement with my childhood faith too. This went hand-in-hand with loss of belief in the inevitability or even likelihood of salvation through the various rationalistic beliefs I had espoused in turn: Marxism, psycho-

ROBERT REINER

analysis, etc. However just as during the period in which I was a firm
believer in atheism, I maintained the Golden Rule ethic of my
religious upbringing, my loss of faith in the prospects of humanistic
progress did not shake my moral and emotional commitment to the
values of social justice as embodied both in the prophetic and the
socialist traditions. In essence I would now regard myself as a Jewish
version of a Christian Socialist: a bagel-eating Blairite.

The concerns derived from my personal background and
experiences now directly influence my work on the police, crime
trends, and my current research on the media and crime, in a way
that was absent in my early years in criminology. Many critics of the
perspective which affects *The politics of the police* have pointed out
that it reflects a Golden Ageism of the type which Geoff Pearson
is supposed to have discredited definitively in his seminal study
Hooligan (Pearson 1983). The book is structured around an account of
what I call the rise and fall of police legitimacy, with the high point
being the 1950s. As these were my childhood and early teenage
years, characterizing this as Paradise Lost fits uncomfortably with
Geoff Pearson's demonstration that middle-aged, middle-class,
middle-everything men like me have always characterized the years
of their youth as a lost Golden Age.

For many years I was touchy on this criticism, generally
wriggling out of it by claiming that I was talking of the 1950s as a
high point in public perceptions of the police (as represented by
survey and other evidence) not a Golden Age in terms of police
practice or any other objective aspects of life. However, since the
publication of *The politics of the police* in 1985 I have been influenced
by several key books which have persuaded me to come out and
argue that the 1950s and 60s were a sort of Golden Age in objective
terms, and that certainly in the early 1970s something happened to
set in motion a general – though not unambiguous – decline in the
quality of life.

The first work to give me the confidence to feel that this perception was not just a reflection of my own hardening arteries was
Alistair MacIntyre's *After virtue* (MacIntyre 1981), which has influenced me more than any other book of the last quarter century.
This persuaded me that the culture of the Enlightenment of which I
had been a true believing disciple in my teens and early adulthood

ROBERT REINER

analysis, etc. However just as during the period in which I was a firm believer in atheism, I maintained the Golden Rule ethic of my religious upbringing, my loss of faith in the prospects of humanistic progress did not shake my moral and emotional commitment to the values of social justice as embodied both in the prophetic and the socialist traditions. In essence I would now regard myself as a Jewish version of a Christian Socialist: a bagel-eating Blairite.

The concerns derived from my personal background and experiences now directly influence my work on the police, crime trends, and my current research on the media and crime, in a way that was absent in my early years in criminology. Many critics of the perspective which affects *The politics of the police* have pointed out that it reflects a Golden Ageism of the type which Geoff Pearson is supposed to have discredited definitively in his seminal study *Hooligan* (Pearson 1983). The book is structured around an account of what I call the rise and fall of police legitimacy, with the high point being the 1950s. As these were my childhood and early teenage years, characterizing this as Paradise Lost fits uncomfortably with Geoff Pearson's demonstration that middle-aged, middle-class, middle-everything men like me have always characterized the years of their youth as a lost Golden Age.

For many years I was touchy on this criticism, generally wriggling out of it by claiming that I was talking of the 1950s as a high point in public perceptions of the police (as represented by survey and other evidence) not a Golden Age in terms of police practice or any other objective aspects of life. However, since the publication of *The politics of the police* in 1985 I have been influenced by several key books which have persuaded me to come out and argue that the 1950s and 60s were a sort of Golden Age in objective terms, and that certainly in the early 1970s something happened to set in motion a general – though not unambiguous – decline in the quality of life.

The first work to give me the confidence to feel that this perception was not just a reflection of my own hardening arteries was Alistair MacIntyre's *After virtue* (MacIntyre 1981), which has influenced me more than any other book of the last quarter century. This persuaded me that the culture of the Enlightenment of which I had been a true believing disciple in my teens and early adulthood

96

contained a time-bomb. It carried the seeds of a relativism about moral discourse which was beginning to threaten the secular humanisms and the related belief – in and to an extent the actuality of – progress which had been the master trend of the first two centuries after the Enlightenment. This triggered an interest in the burgeoning literature about post-modernity which is reflected in much of my recent writing on the police, notably my inaugural lecture (Reiner 1992b).

The other works which have influenced me greatly of late are Eric Hobsbawm's magisterial history of the "short" twentieth century *Age of extremes* (Hobsbawm 1994), Will Hutton's analysis of our economic woes *The state we are in* (Hutton 1995) and David Rose's account of the "collapse of criminal justice" *In the name of the law* (Rose 1996). Between them these give me confidence that the perspective which underlies my recent work on trends in crime is supportable (Reiner 1996a, b). For all the caveats about statistics and moral panics, crime has risen since the 1950s, and in particular since the late 1970s. It is a major issue in its own right but also the most visible symbol of deeper malaise, economic, social and cultural. This is reflected in the mass media representation of crime and violence (and possibly aggravated by it in turn: Livingstone 1996; Reiner 1996c). My current interests all reflect this. The research project on changing media images of crime since the Second World War on which I am engaged on with Sonia Livingstone and Jessica Allen is a direct product of my concern to analyse these changes. So too are my continuing interests in trying to understand current trends in crime, control, policing and security, which will be embodied in my next edition of *The politics of the police* and various articles.

I have never had trouble accepting Gramsci's recommendation of pessimism of the intellect. I have chronic problems with the associated encouragement of optimism of the will. My basic perspective certainly suggests that at present civilization is fighting a losing battle with barbarism. However, I remain unquenchably optimistic about the capacity of reason, research and scholarship to illuminate the sources of this and point ways forward. (I am not just pitching to the ESRC for a research grant.) Criminology can interpret the world, and if recent Home Secretaries can change it for the worse, it is possible for others to change it for the better.

CHAPTER 6

Back to the future: the predictive value of social theories of delinquency

David Downes

The social and economic landscape today is widely regarded as subject to tumultuous change unprecedented in its speed and seemingly uncontrollable direction since the first Industrial Revolution of the 1780s. At the same time, it is eerily familiar. Ghosts long since thought of as laid have returned to haunt us, in the shape of the shrouded figures of the homeless, the outstretched hands of beggars and municipal graves for the nameless dead. It is increasingly the case that these developments are regarded as the sad, but inevitable accompaniments to late or post modernity, whose results are viewed as immensely beneficial to the minority but unfortunately slow to reach the groups variously described as the "excluded", the "underclass" or the "bottom tenth" (or "fifth" or "third", depending on whatever index is used). These trends have been astonishingly sudden in their impact, it is claimed, taking governments and experts by surprise. None can be blamed for their happening, since no-one predicted their occurrence. Moreover, it is often implied that the plight of the excluded is an unwanted but inevitable price worth paying for progress.

As a child of the welfare state, a number of the first generation to be the beneficiaries of post-war social planning, I am both angered and saddened by this debacle. It was both avoidable and predictable. Changes had to come but they could have been handled far better, more humanely and less divisively. My perspective on these changes is stamped by growing up in the city of Sheffield, which enjoyed a 35-year-long period of prosperous full employment before the era of wanton job destruction began in 1980–81. My father worked as a labour manager in a large steel firm. We were a Conservative family in an overwhelmingly Labour town. Yet we lived on a Council estate with no sense of stigma. The social mix on such estates was far greater then than now, and the sense of community we enjoyed I encountered again only decades later on visiting Israeli communes. The National Health Service in general dealt perfectly well with illness, though GPs were over-burdened, and visits to surgery took hours. Only in education was there a sense of social fracture. Passing the 11-plus exam took me across the city to "King Ted's", the grammar school about which a friend said, "Tha'll never gerrin theer." Immediately, a social chasm opened up. In Sheffield, more than any other city in England, social class is spatially concentrated.

Crime was virtually unknown on this estate, though my sympathies for Geoff Pearson's argument in *Hooligan* (1983) stem from knowing that street fights took place, of a minor kind and never involving weapons, which nowadays would lead to police action. We enjoyed as children a freedom of the streets now unimaginable, partly due to the new found fear of crime but mainly due to fear of traffic. So my entry into criminology was not inspired by personal experience of delinquency. It was largely a process of drift.

At Oxford, I had studied history, but as then taught, it stopped at 1914 and gave little purchase on the modern world. That engagement largely came through films and novels. The American cinema of the 1950s, along with a lot of junk, threw up a sequence of films that bristled with acute social awareness: *Marty, The Bachelor Party, End As A Man* and that most prescient of films *The Sweet Smell of Success*. European cinema had also developed, through Italian neo-realism in particular a concern for ordinary lives, whether of the old, the marginal or the drifter, which was conveyed with astonishing virtuosity. Seeing de Sica's *Bicycle Thieves* and *Umberto D.* and Fellini's *La Strada, I Vitelloni Il Bidone* and *Cabiria* for the first time were formative experiences. Among other things, the damage often wrought on ordinary lives by even petty crime, for both victim *and* offender in different ways, is conveyed quite unforgettably. Also, crime is in these films never shown as flowing from individual pathology, but from the interplay of biography, personal situation and social context, which are conveyed with luminous artistry. No-one in these films is an extra or a stereotype, in the crassly patronizing and wooden mode of so many British films of the period, in a cinema stifled by J. Arthur Rank. The British cinema was to learn the lesson and turn out fine films as a result, largely based on the novels of the period which broke the hold of the old Establishment for good: *Room at the top*, *Saturday night and Sunday morning* and *This sporting life* in particular.

So, from the word go, I was what would now be termed a Left Realist in criminology, or maybe a Left Neo-Realist, before even entering the field, and not even knowing of the existence of the subject. It was by chance that I discovered it. Writing to the London School of Economics for a social work place (out of a vague sense of do-goodery and not knowing that this was to be the department in which I would spend most of my working life), I enquired about related courses. Asher Tropp of the department of sociology wrote to ask if I had considered research in criminology. I met him and learnt that people did research into such subjects as drug taking, white collar crime and delinquency (these turned out to be Edwin Schur, Gerald Mars and Terence Morris). I was astonished to learn of these possibilities and immediately signed on.

From these somewhat frivolous beginnings came serious effects. I was supervised by Terence Morris (and, to his eternal credit, by Eryl Hall-William) and quickly brought to grapple with the dire state of criminology in Britain, recently savaged by Barbara Wootton in her *Social science and social pathology* (1959). I ploughed through the mish-mash of cod psychology and social factor theory with a heavy heart. Where was the sense in all of this of meaning, motive and context? Fortunately the sociology of crime in Britain was burgeoning with the work of John Mays, Herman Mannheim and Terence Morris himself. His combination of passion and rigour was on a plane entirely new to me, and things were undoubtedly stirring. We had had the rock 'n' roll riots, the Teddy Boy Movement and a rising rate of crime and delinquency which defied explanation in sheer deprivation terms, given the growth of prosperity in the past decade. The only theories to make real sense were American. In testing out those theories in a British context, the East End of London, I had to conclude that the class system in Britain, while accounting for much delinquency, also exercised powerful constraints against its metamorphosis into something worse. But the character of class and its political representation were not static and changes would be forced upon them, unless some political direction was given to how those changes would be handled for the best.

Sadly, the Labour governments that won power 1964–70 on the promise of applying the white heat of technology to social problems never applied that insight in the key areas of further education and industrial training. In a long forgotten Fabian report *Educating for uncertainty* (1965), Fred Flower (then Principal of Kingsway College, the pioneer of much that was best in FE) and I argued the case for a major expansion of this (still) neglected sector (Downes and Flower 1965). If Jennie Lee, the creator of the Open University, had taken hold of the issue, she might have transformed the situation. As it was, all energies were directed to the transition to comprehensive secondary education and the new polytechnics. Labour's defeat in the 1970 election, the most important political event since 1945, was largely due to the rejection of Barbara Castle's attempt, as the ministerial architect of the 1969 White Paper, *In place of strife*, to resolve the growing problem of industrial conflict. It spelt the end of the "Butskellite" consensus and the start of the political sea change which ushered in the New Right era. The problem – how to handle technological change without dire social and economic consequences – was to become the solution – the use of technology to shed labour and maximize profits. The results are all too plain. They should not be seen as the inevitable result of immutable trends but as the at least partly avoidable results of the short-termism of both Left and Right from the late 1960s.

The political situation today is consequently grave. Since 1979, the pillars of the welfare state have been systematically and severely eroded. The components of a kind of market fascism have been assembled: through job destruction policies and the growth of job insecurity; through regressive taxation; through growing disenchantment at local level by the weakening of local authorities; through the increase in poverty, inequality and social exclusion; and through the growing power of media moguls such as Rupert Murdoch. One hesitates to use the term *fascism*, with its apocalyptic overtones in a period which is not only fin de siècle but fin de millennium. But it registers the looming reality of Durkheim's dictum that a society in which nothing intervenes between a hypertrophied state and a mass of disaggregated individuals is a veritable sociological monstrosity. From being too developed, trade union rights are now near extinction. The USA is well ahead in this development: with nearly 2,000,000 prisoners, severe limits on the powers of the judiciary, zero tolerance policing and new forms of social exclusion and surveillance. But we are not far behind. It is not too late to pull back from this abyss, and the coming election may begin the process. But it is dangerously close.

The view from 1965

In 1965, by contrast, the social mood was one of marked optimism that, as long as the path of steady reform was pursued, all could increasingly be well for all, not simply the majority. This was the world of social democratic hope, with the way ahead for youth mapped by a stream of official inquiries which had begun with the Crowther Report (1959) on the education of 15–18-year-olds and the Albemarle Report (1960) on the Youth Service. Widespread acceptance of gradualism as the appropriate strategy prevailed across the political spectrum, for all but the tiny revolutionary left and the minority hard right. The major political parties differed chiefly in the mix they preferred economically between public and private sectors, the scale of welfare services rather than their character, and the size of the defence budget. Though the era of "Butskellite" consensus was entering its last decade, technological change was seen as almost entirely benign in its social and economic effects. Harold Wilson and the Labour Party won the General Election of 1964 partly as the result of their success in linking Labour with the "white heat of technology". Even at this high point of modernity, however, with full employment, growing welfare provision and busy assembly lines, clear warnings were struck about the worsening social problems that would result from unchecked inequalities and the growth of consumerism.

Particularly prescient were J.K. Galbraith's famous contrast between private affluence and public squalor in *The affluent society* (1959); Richard Titmuss's analysis (1960) of the growing power of private pension funds as a new force for irresponsibility in society (socially irresponsible and politically unaccountable precisely because their legal responsibilities were solely to maximize profits for their client groups); and Tosco Fyvel's stress, in a study of the social context of new forms of delinquency, *The insecure offenders* (1961), on the role of advertising as making for social unbalance, since the advertising industry – echoing Galbraith – massively boosted private goods, rarely public services. Michael Young's brilliant dystopia *The rise of the meritocracy* (1958) showed how the reforms of the 1944 Education Act would logically lead not to a diminishing of inequalities but to a change in their character. Colin MacInnes was almost the sole guide to the efflorescence of youth culture, whose obsessive beguilement with clothes, fashion, music and style he explored in *Absolute beginners* (1959) and *England half English* (MacInnes 1961). These books conveyed a sense of social change, cultural possibilities and economic dangers with which one had to wrestle.

Another prescient strand singled out automation as the key to late twentieth century development. Such books as Denis Gabor's *Inventing the future* (1963) and Robert Blauner's *Alienation and freedom* (1964) defined the challenge of automation as requiring alertness to its potential for either blighting or enhancing the character of work, depending on the choices that were made about its uses. There was in the late 1950s and early 1960s a great deal of popular awareness of automation. Fyvel quoted one of his youthful delinquents as saying: "extra school won't get a boy any place. Automation's coming. That means more jobs for a few people with brains and for the rest the same thing all day" (Fyvel 1961: 120). This statement contained two tragic misconceptions: that school therefore did not matter, and that the same thing rather than nothing would ensue. Perhaps the most interesting point, however, is the widespread awareness that human labour was about to be radically affected on a massive scale by automation. This perception came to be overlaid in the late 1960s, 70s and well into the 1980s by short-term anxieties about industrial conflict and inflation. As a result, the revolution in information technology was allowed to just happen. Two decades of preparing the ground for its immense consequences were lost, so that they are now experienced in terms of new form of determinism and defeatism.

Taken together, these strands have proved quite accurate

predictors of what has since occurred, unevenly but persistently across the Western industrialized world. Private affluence has grown significantly in the last few decades, notably over the past 15 years, but the growth of inequality mars the picture. Examples abound of huge discrepancies between the top salaries in the private sector, now swollen by the privatization of large chunks of former public sector utilities and services and the pay of routine staff. The rise in affluence for all but the highest earners is also exaggerated by trend figures which routinely take income net of tax as the key index, a trick of accountancy which excludes the need to pay, out of post-tax income for a host of services decreasingly met from taxation, such as student maintenance, school equipment, health prescriptions and housing costs. Indirect taxation is in effect counted as income *gain*. Public squalor has ramified in ways unanticipated by even the gloomiest social commentator of the 1960s. The resurgence of beggary and homelessness; the return pre-war diseases as tuberculosis (recently documented in an excellent series of articles on the East End by the London *Evening Standard* (The Betrayed 16–20 1/95)); the explosion of new forms of drug abuse; the emergence of mass unemployment on a scale thought irreconcilable with good economic management after World War Two; and the recrudescence of socially excluded (or underclass) groups, again on a scale once deemed unimaginable in the context of modern welfare services. "Public squalor", unemployment and social exclusion in Britain today are now in key respects on a scale and of a character convergent with those of the USA, a comparison which would have seemed alarmist in the 1960s.

Of the other indicators of social unbalance cited by Fyvel, Titmuss and Galbraith, advertising has since 1965 undergone a massive expansion, intensification and growth in sophistication, a phenomenon largely unexplored by sociologists, if beloved of semioticians. A key symbol of its sway is the appropriation by advertisers of songs that were once the symbol of youthful rebellion. Desmond Dekker's "The Israelites" now advertises Vitalite. The pensions industry has grown hugely as a force in investment and economic influence. One-third of all stock is now owned by pension funds, compared with 12 per cent in 1957 (*The Guardian* 7/1/95; Titmuss, 1960: 14, Note 1). As its *sole* interest lies in maximum profits, increasingly bought at the expense of full-time employment, its contribution to the "irresponsible society" has correspondingly magnified. And auto-mation, now renamed the revolution in information technology, has – almost everywhere except Japan – been deployed to replace huge numbers of jobs. The rise of *non*-employment alongside employ-ment; the replacement of full-time, permanent, unionized work by part-time, temporary, non-unionized jobs; the growth of household inequality due to the rise of dual-earning households and that of non-earning households: all these trends have combined to produce growing economic and job insecurities which increasingly affect middle-class as well as working-class employees. Best captured in Lea and Young's matchless phrase "if the first Industrial Revolution rested on the exploitation of Labour by capital, the second is based on the 'emancipation' of capital from Labour" (Lea and Young, 1984:3) This emancipation is largely fuelled by the search for short-term profits. It is facilitated by governmental policies of deregulation and privatization, which are accomplished by the new managerialist strategies of de-layering and contracting out. At the corporate level, take-overs, buyouts and mergers leave employees (and often managers) defenceless against asset-stripping and job-shedding. Popular analyses are now beginning to appear which document the unusual extent to which Anglo–American capitalism is wedded to such practices, by comparison with other western European and the Japanese economies (Hutton 1995), coupled with the irony that the social damage wrought has not even paid off in term of economic growth (Rowntree 1995).

The character and magnitude of these changes are often now seen, even on the new Marxist Left, as inevitable post-Fordist adjustments to the condition of post-modernity (see Harvey 1990 for an exhaustive discussion of the debate). Yet, even accepting the irreversibility of the revolution in information technology, the scope it affords for shedding labour, and the likely irreversibility of changing gender relations in the family and occupationally, there still remain a host of developments, in Britain in particular, which are the outcome of political choice rather than economic necessity. In Britain, what amount to job destruction policies are exemplified in the virtual extinction of the mining industry; in the closure of large parts of the steel industry (the last major plant closure at Ravenscraig in 1993) neatly coincided with the onset of a recovery which necessitated steel imports); and in the freezing of receipts from council house sales, which entailed the near abandonment of fresh local authority building. Huge state investment has instead been fed to such Enterprise Zone projects as London Docklands whose infrastructure has been developed at the expense of local firms whose jobs have been lost or displaced in the process (Docklands Forum 1990; on the failure of the Urban Development Corporation strategy in general, see Deakin 1995). A final example of change which resulted from choice rather than necessity is the Poll Tax of 1988, a disastrously misconceived experiment which led to the census under-count of over a million citizens in 1991 (Heady et al. 1994), an index of sharply growing disaffection and civil exclusion. The main group to evade census enumeration were men between 18 and 30 including the growing number of homeless youths who – again in the face of clear advice from authoritative sources – the government chose to relieve of the burden of Housing Benefit. These are not essential or inevitable results of "late modernity" but outcomes of what Titmuss called the "irresponsible" and David Marquand termed the "unprincipled" society (1988): that is, they are on different moral and economic principles, *avoidable*. They gravely and needlessly aggravated what would anyway have been a most difficult transition to a more automated economy less dependent on sheer muscle-power and traditional skills.

The criminological implications of these developments over the past two or three decades have been set out by sociologists from Durkheim onwards, and especially by Robert Merton and the subcultural theorists who variously followed his basic model. As the main problem seemed to me in 1960 to revolve around how to account for rising rates of delinquency *despite* growing affluence, social stability and welfare support, these authors – Robert Merton, Albert Cohen, Richard Cloward and David Matza – proved seminal influences. Merton in particular seemed to fasten onto the crucial variable – the fostering of the propensity to consume as a pre-condition for capitalist expansion. This entails the revolution of rising expectations, a process which is perfectly acceptable as long as people in general have some reasonable chance of meeting them. To the extent that they do not, this institutionalized dissatisfaction takes its toll. With hindsight, Merton had taken one component of Marx's analysis of capitalist political economy and distilled a theory of deviance from its implications. Despite his borrowing of the term

107

anomie from Durkheim, he is far more Marxist than Durkheimian in his analysis, though it is a secularized and filleted Marxism, not the full-blown thesis. For this reason, Merton has not proved popular among Marxists, despite these affinities.

Merton's basic contention was that the strain towards anomie (and high rates of deviance) was built into any society which held certain goals to be available to all but withheld access to them from the majority. The problem is particularly acute for democracies, which are, however remotely, based on an egalitarian ethic; and – in the American case – uniquely so, because a consumer culture stresses, above all else the goal of money success. In the post-World War II era, subcultural theorists such as Albert Cohen and Richard Cloward adapted this framework to address the problem of the continuing rise in crime and delinquency rates despite growing affluence. In particular, they saw the source of gang delinquency as stemming from the experience of relative deprivation in the schools and in the job market respectively. Essentially, growing affluence combined with persistent inequalities would generate increasing rates of deviance. Moreover, structural changes were under way which would heighten rather than reduce inequalities. In 1963, Cloward wrote that, due to the shrinking occupational structure for manual work, the streets of our urban slums are slowly filling with young men who have no prospect of finding manhood through work, who are coming of age in a society that neither wants nor needs them. John Mays predicted in 1964 that if inequality remained unchecked in the context of growing affluence, crime rates would double within 25 years. He was wrong about the magnitude of the rise – they trebled – but right about the direction.

In similar vein, following a comparative study of delinquency in London's East End, I concluded that if the non-skilled young are to be denied the chance of engaging in building a technological society, as well as benefiting from it, the price they exact will be high (Downes, 1966:16). In other words, what was in prospect, if such problems were not addressed, was not just more of the same, but a shift in the character of delinquency to the American pattern. My interpretation of the theories was that they worked quite well, when applied to Britain, to account for the then much milder forms and levels of crime and delinquency in this country compared to the USA. The theories of David Matza on delinquency and drift, on "subterranean values" and on techniques of neutralization, seemed to account best for such changes in delinquency as were occurring in Britain. In particular, his conception of delinquency as the manufacture of excitement in the limbo of adolescence, seemed to me to capture the character of youthful defiance and deviance extraordinarily well. It lacked only one key element – the greater involvement in delinquency of the least advantaged working-class youth – which I sought to supply through the twofold notion of leisure as the all-important arena for young men to assert themselves on the one hand, and the impact of youth culture in raising their expectations of fulfilment in leisure, rather than school or work on the other. But the earlier theorists had supplied the main ingredients of the *comparative* variations between the USA and Britain. Three variables seemed crucial in explaining that difference: (1) the nature of class formations in Britain, and their political representation, reduced the strain to anomie; (2) more modest aspirations were channelled collectively rather than individually, with cultural emphasis placed more on full employment and welfare institutions rather than on individual upward mobility and success; and (3) ethnic loyalties did not fragment class allegiances. These conditions for what amounted to a massive set of informal controls against more serious levels of crime and delinquency have all been fractured by the social and economic changes cited above. More than 30 years on have the consequences matched the theoretical predictions? Has the recipe for anomie worked?

Outcome in 1995

In some respects, the results are fully in line with predictions. Rates of crime against property in England and Wales are now as high, in some cases higher than in the USA. They are also (except in the Multinational Crime Surveys) higher than in The Netherlands and, since 1980, have risen more steeply than in Scotland. There are grounds for thinking that, though rates of crime against property have risen steadily in virtually all industrial societies over the past four decades, they have risen more precipitously in this country than in virtually all others. This trend is all the more remarkable because, at least for the past 10–15 years, most forms of movable property have been locked, bolted and barred either physically or electronically to a quite unprecedented degree – so much so that the crime rate is now increasingly a displacement rate. Forms of electronic surveillance such as closed-circuit television (CCTV) have also pervaded most forms of public space, to an extent which would be deemed Orwellian but for the success with which the discourse of crime control has neutralized opposition. Even so, continental criminologists have commented on the ease with which such measures have been introduced in Britain; in countries with a history of fascist occupation, they are more vigorously contested. They have yet to pay off in terms of lasting crime reduction, despite some temporary such effects. As it is, crime rates have quintupled since the mid-1960s and more than doubled since 1979. Nor, as Waddington has stressed (1986) can this simply be written off as a 5–6 per cent average annual rise since World War I. In absolute terms, a 5 per cent rise in the 1990s equals 250,000 more offences annually, i.e. half of the total of recorded crimes in the mid-1950s.

A second change in line with predictions is the rise in illicit drug use of all kinds since the 1960. While some of this was due to the widespread acceptance of marijuana (and other recreational drugs, such as Ecstasy) across all classes by the young, some at least can be attributed to two avoidable factors: first, long-term youth un-employment, largely a working-class affliction, and secondly the unforced abandonment of the British system of heroin maintenance programmes by the mid-1970s. Whatever its flaws, the so-called British system of maintenance prescribing for registered heroin addicts by medical practitioners undercut the black market in the highly profitable opiate trade. The lurch into chronic levels of long-term youth unemployment brought to an end the era in which such addiction was kept within medically manageable proportions. It will be infinitely more difficult to reconstruct policies which were formerly in place and viable, but it will still ultimately have to be done, albeit now at vastly greater cost, otherwise drug trafficking and related crime will increasingly wreck humane penal policies, policing and the politics of law and order.

Violence is the big exception to predictions based on anomie and subcultural theories. Given the structural change in youth un-employment, growing economic inequality and social polarization, the predictable outcome in large urban areas should have been the development of more violent forms of gang delinquency in the context of rising violence in general. Some signs of such shifts *have* occurred over the past decade, for example, sporadic reports of drug-related gang warfare in Moss Side, Manchester; fashions in group delinquency such as "steaming", "hotting" and "ram-raiding" in estates as diverse as Meadowell in Tyneside and Blackbird Leys in Oxford; and outbreaks of racial violence in the East and Southeast of London. But such developments are not as yet subject to sociological, as distinct from journalistic reportage, and seem too ill-substantiated to bear any stronger interpretation than that they are temporary alignments (however unpleasant) rather than permanent changes.

Two changes that do seem to have become part of the social landscape are rioting and prolonged delinquent careers. The first wave of riots began in St. Paul's, Bristol, in 1980 and seemed to peter out after the murder of PC Blakelock at Broadwater Farm in 1985. As in the Brixton riots of 1981, these were triggered by incidents taken to be symbolic of police harassment of black minority youth. Subsequent waves of rioting were more diverse, at times stemming from similar flashpoints, but also including the anti-Poll Tax riot of 1988; those against the export of veal calves in the mid-1990s; anti-road building demonstrations and occupations; and a number of riotous events on estates not particularly marked by severe social problems. The common threads seem to be a potent sense of grievance and the felt lack of political representation.

The prolongation of delinquent careers is again in line with predictions, though evidence for this trend is incomplete. The peak age for officially recorded delinquency shifted during the 1980s from the almost hallowed figure for males of school-leaving minus one, i.e. 14 until 1972, 15 after the raising of the school-leaving age in that year, but now it is 18. In a self-report survey of "Young people and crime" (1995), the most striking finding was that 27 per cent of males aged 22–25 admitted to current offences against property compared with 17 per cent and 25 per cent in the 14–17 and 18–21 age-groups. For women, the figures in order of descending age were 3, 9, and 13 per cent, far more in line with the conventional wisdom that offending reaches its peak in mid-adolescence and thereafter declines. For males, this finding is consistent with the prolongation of delinquency into the mid-20s at least. Unfortunately, no time series exists by which to assess how far this trend is entirely novel. Thirdly, some recent field study suggests that prolongation is real, relatively new and related to joblessness. The transition from delinquency to marriage and a steady job has been wiped out for many by the disappearance of jobs of the minimum quality needed to support a family. The predicted consequences for delinquency and crime have now materialized.

Violence in general *has*, according to police statistics, risen consistently with broad predictions, but its character has not changed as a corollary. Nor are all observers agreed that even violence in general has increased. Chris Nuttall, head of the Criminal Statistics Division of the Home Office, has argued that, domestic violence excepted (whose rise is arguably due to changes in police reactions rather than to any real change), national victim surveys between 1981 and 1992 show no rise in crimes of violence at all. (The 1993 survey did show a slight rise, however.) Such a non-development is in line with two persuasive theses. The first is that violence has been declining since the first records of homicide can be traced with regularity, from the thirteenth century, when murder rates were vastly higher than today. Since 1950, however, rates of violence have worsened, and one explanation is that the change is more to do with decreasing tolerance of even minor acts of aggression than occurred in the recent past. Boys' fights, for example, or late night public brawls, which in the 1930s would have been defined as normal acts of masculine prowess or customary ways of settling disputes, would now be cues for phoning the police. Such a view is in line with the celebrated theory of Norbert Elias, that long-term trends in civil society have led to the development of psychic self-controls sufficiently strong to offset social changes that may otherwise have made for more violent interpersonal relations (1978).

Against that view, certain caveats should be noted. First, as Oliver James (1995) has argued, the British Crime Survey figures may be poor estimates of crime against the person (as distinct from those against property), since the groups most involved are under-sampled and under-respond. One such group, boys under the age of 16, are not sampled at all. Secondly, the fall of 1,000,000 in the most violence-prone age group is not allowed for in the BCS estimates and may be a demographic reason for at least some of the reduced rise in violence in the victim surveys. Thirdly, certain groups with a heightened risk of violence, e.g. young, homeless males, have both increased in size over the past two decades and have effectively and increasingly dropped out of civil society altogether. They appear neither in census returns nor in BCS sample frame. There are over 1,000,000 civic dropouts, the Poll Tax being a major reason for their submergence. Fourthly, social polarization and ghettoization have now reached such extreme in both the UK and the USA that police reportage is an increasingly flawed reflection of real crime. This is one possible explanation of the levelling off of reported violent crime rates in the USA, where such developments exceed those in western Europe in general. Telephone surveys are especially suspect as correctives to official data on this front. Such "crime warps" obscure real trends.

These *are*, however, caveats rather than established facts, and could only be taken further by systematic social ethnographies of the sort that seem to have gone out of fashion. (Exceptions exist – the work of Hobbs (1988) and Foster (1990) – only confirms this general trend.) On balance, one can only conclude that, despite massive strains to the social-fabric, declining levels of trust and greater insecurity, the level and character of violence, though quantitatively somewhat worse, seem *qualitatively* little changed since the 1960s (Northern Ireland excepted).

It would not do, however, to rest easy on the theses of Elias and the trend data of the BCS. All the components for such a qualitative shift towards more patterned violence are now in place. One signal change, increasingly well documented, is the emergence of the so-called "underclass" of the excluded. From Bea Campbell's *Goliath* (1993) and her notion of a "crisis in masculinity" to Charles Murray's caricature of the "new rabble" (1994), diverse analyses are being offered of a fundamental sea-change in the social structure of western societies. The whole underclass debate, and the career of the concept, reflect the marginalization of academics other than those of the "new right". The underclass concept was first used in Britain by Ralf Dahrendorf (1987), who expressed unease in the mid-1980s at the emergence of long-term unemployment and its likely social consequences. It was taken up for a time across the political spectrum. However, as if to confirm the argument of John Macnicol (1987) that the concept has in the past and will in the future be appropriated eugenically by the ultra-right, Charles Murray was given unprecedented coverage by a major newspaper, the *Sunday Times*, to develop his thesis that high and rising crime stemmed from rising illegitimacy rates which, in turn, were caused by welfare dependency. Murray's latest offering, *The bell curve*, written with Richard Herrnstein, (1994) comes right on cue to fulfil Macnicol's prediction.

Empirical support for either link in this chain is weak in the extreme. There is no sound evidence, once poverty and social background factors are controlled for, that single parenthood, let alone illegitimacy, is causally responsible for delinquency. It is the factors that are controlled for that are likely to be causally implicated (Rutter and Giller 1983), there is no good evidence that levels of welfare benefit are causally implicated in rates of illegitimacy. Christopher Jencks in the USA concluded a major review of the evidence by stating, "Welfare benefits do not provide a very convincing explanation for unwed motherhood" (Jencks and Peterson 1991).

Cross-national data collated by David Piachaud suggest little connection between these variables. In Denmark, Belgium, Germany, France and The Netherlands, single-parent benefit as a percentage of average earnings ranges from 30 to 65 per cent higher than in the UK, yet lone-parent families as a percentage of all families with children under 18 are 12 to 50 per cent *lower* (see NACRO 1995). If Murray is right, exactly the reverse should hold true. Other aspects of the links in the Murray chain are contested on American data by Freeman; Osterman; and Duncan and Hoffman (Jencks and Peterson op. cit.). Yet Murray has won the political debate. Benefits for unwed mothers are being cut back in the USA and in the UK. The strains to anomie are evident in the very conduct of academic debate and its public impact.

All of which brings one to new sites for anomie, the realm of policy-making and the politics of law and order. Without wishing to elevate the Home Office of the 1960s to Golden Age stature, the approach to policy-making in the era of Rab Butler and Roy Jenkins was one of rational pragmatism. The escapes of Biggs and Blake led to Mountbatten's inquiry and, even though his recommendations were overturned by the subsequent report of the Radzinowicz committee, both were informed by the recognition that prisons were under-secure for 5 per cent and over-secure for 95 per cent of their population. Getting the prison population down or at least stabilized was a policy aim that led to the 1967 Parole Act and to the innovations of community service and suspended sentences in the 1970s. That these reforms proved ineffective and to some extent backfired is well-known, developments which led in the 1980s to the surprising and unpredicted construction of a strategy of decarceration (Cavadino and Dignan 1992).

1980 proved to be a period of informed penal policy-making that was sustained in the teeth of a set of circumstances hostile to decarceration; crime rates rose seemingly inexorably until 1987–8, when they fell slightly; anxiety about public order mounted due to the new wave of rioting and conflict on several industrial relations fronts; and both the fear of crime and the extent of victimization were charted by the British Crime Surveys and several at local level, all of which fed into an increasingly heated media coverage. And yet, in spite and to some extent, because of the space won by punitive government rhetoric, successive Conservative Home Secretaries became convinced of (at times converted to) the wisdom of a reductionist penal strategy. More than rhetoric was involved, however; in 1984, Leon Brittan announced the biggest prison building programme since the nineteenth century, and the right to parole was effectively withdrawn from offenders imprisoned for four years or more for offences of violence and drug-trafficking. At the same time, the ground was being laid by a group of senior civil servants, notably David Faulkner, for an alternative strategy to incessant increases in the prison population. The guiding thread was the assembly of a convincing set of non-penal alternatives in community sanctions, crime prevention and victim support. The climax of all this activity was the 1991 Criminal Justice Act, the key elements of which had been extensively canvassed and market tested with key groups of criminal justice practitioners during the previous three years. The Woolf Report of the same year had set the scene for legislation which stabilized the prison population whilst its recommendations, accepted by the government, were put into effect.

That the 1991 Act was flawed in two respects was no excuse for the shambles which followed the 1992 election. The flaws in the clauses concerning previous convictions and unit fines, both of which were remediable were taken as the pretext by Kenneth Clarke and Michael Howard to reverse a decade of cumulative and coherent policy-making across the whole criminal justice field. By his proclamation that "Prison works" at the 1993 Conservative Party Conference, Michael Howard signalled his intention not only to talk the prison population up, but also to legislate for a substantial rise. So striking a U-turn demands explanation in terms other than the need to combat crime, which had served as the ostensible motive for the policy which had been overturned. Three motives may be suspected. First, the steep rise in crime 1989–92 had seen the Labour Party take an unprecedented lead over the Conservatives as better able to deal with law and order in public opinion polls; and Tony Blair, then the Shadow Home Secretary, had coined his phrase that policy should be "tough on crime, tough on the causes of crime". To be upstaged by Labour, for so long the butt of the Conservatives as "soft on crime", must have been anathema to the Tories. Reversion to type was called for. Labour must bear some responsibility for this debacle, because their criticism of the Tories focused on the leniency of punishment rather than the social and economic sources of crime, in particular the strong association between the 1989–92 increase and the depth and length of the recession. Secondly, privatization in the prison sphere would be greatly assisted by the creation of new prisons that could be justified by greater numbers of prisoners. Thirdly, the scope for privatization would help to break the power of the Prison Officers' Association, a nagging survival from the 1980s' assault on the bases of union strength. As Nils Christie has argued, prison privatization is proving a force for expanding prisons as industries and as a source of profits.

The resulting anomie in policy-making is well exemplified by the shouldering aside of the Department of Health by the Home Office in the plan to create 200 new secure unit places for young offenders; in the sacking of Derek Lewis, head of the newly formed Prisons Agency for his alleged responsibility for the escapes from Parkhurst Prison; by the evident collapse of morale in the Home Office; and by the haste with which commercialized forms of privatization have been pushed through in the prison sector. A quite unprecedented antipathy came to be expressed towards the Home Secretary by every branch of the criminal justice system, as in the Lord Chief Justice's forceful opposition to mandatory sentencing proposals, police criticism at the adoption of crude performance indicators of the effectiveness of policing; and the suggestion that the pay of probation officers should be linked with their "success" in reforming criminals. Well established procedures for policy process in the Home Office have been drastically eroded (Rock 1995).

Again, in the sphere of the politics of law and order, three decades ago non-partisanship largely prevailed. In our review of how that situation had changed dramatically, Rod Morgan and I (Downes and Morgan 1994) concluded that, although at the time of writing (late 1992) policy remained framed by the 1991 Act, it was clearly subject to increasingly volatile change. This volatility mirrored the experience of the past two decades in the USA, in which the prison population had trebled to become the highest in the Free World. It is now clear that the politics of law and order have imposed themselves on policy-making to an unprecedented degree; and that those politics are increasingly subject to "punitive populism" (Bottoms 1995), a mode of discourse which annihilates any alternative to the blanket use of custody for ever larger swathes of offending. It presages an era of penological machismo, in which the length, weight and depth of imprisonment are traded up in party political contestations of virility, and in which the penetration of disciplinary controls into civic life – screening, surveillance, and security checks – is justified in terms of crime control (Cohen, S. 1985).

A major irony is that criminology in Britain is increasingly marginalized and ignored at the point where its maturity and productivity are most pronounced. In early 1995, for example, Geoff Mulgan cited in *the Guardian* that Charles Murray and James Q. Wilson as intellectual giants compared with their British counterparts. This ludicrous statement shows a sad ignorance of the work of Brian Abel-Smith, David Piachaud and Peter Townsend on poverty and David Garland and Jock Young on punishment and crime. I find this a sad reflection of how far even the quality press has distanced itself from sociology and criminology. This departure presages a new post-modernist superficiality in British intellectual life as reflected in media coverage. It is now more likely that the most important arguments and evidence against the populist view of crime – that it is the product of a feckless underclass spawned by indulgent welfarism – and punishment – that a soaring prison population is a price worth paying for the illusion of its control – will not get a hearing. Perhaps as members of the British Society of Criminology, the nearest we come to a professional association, we should put our minds to how best to address that gulf.

To sum up: the social theories of crime and delinquency of the mid-50s to mid-60s, for all their faults, predicted the shape of things to come surprisingly well. Thirty years from now their message is that, unless we can rediscover something resembling the egalitarian ethic as a guiding principle of social policy, we shall have to endure not only more of the same but markedly worse forms of predatory victimization. Though Mike Davis finds the projected world of *Blade Runner* curiously old-fashioned by comparison with contemporary Los Angeles, it could fit the future for Britain remarkably well. Its director, Ridley Scott, is – after all – British, from Newcastle. It was made in 1978, when the juxtaposition of the gleaming tower of Canary Wharf and the bleak estates of East London were not yet fashioned. Our technological sophistication continues to race ahead of our social inventiveness. Given the trends, it could well be replicants playing cricket and cycling to church, in a security bubble leisure zone, that form the virtual reality of England in 2026, an image beamed to those in the real-world estates of the excluded, electronically fenced off from the privatized homes of the prosperous.

It should be said that, if the root ideas of anomie and subcultural theories which have been reanimated by the development of Left Realism are to last another few decades, then some very belated work needs to be done on their key components. For example, relative deprivation, rightly seen by Jock Young as a cornerstone of the approach, remains astonishingly unexplored empirically by criminologists, and the social and symbolic impact of advertising, despite its central role in the consumer society, awaits sophisticated trend analysis, other than as a system of signs. We know next to nothing about its effects, processing and significance for our ordering of values. We have moved too far away from the causes and political economy of crime as a focus for theory and research, at least in Britain. By contrast, in the USA, the work of John Hagan, Mercer Sullivan, Elliot Currie and several others is bringing ethnographic work to bear on the most critical points of change in the nature of social inequality and crime. Once again, after two decades of hiatus, the USA seem to be producing research and analysis of the kind we most need to conduct.

Note

This chapter is based partly on a seminar paper presented at the British Society of Criminology, January 1995.

CHAPTER 7

Roots of a perspective

Nils Christie

I have been invited to reflect upon ideas that underpin my work, and also to include a discussion of personal intellectual history.[1] The danger in such a task is to become entrapped in the private. To escape that danger, I will attempt to describe how the development of ideas are influenced by the same forces that also influence both crime and forms of crime control. Theories on deviance and theories of theories on deviance might stem from the same root. This does not mean that I see myself as a robot, where my writing is fully determined by the surroundings. Nor do I look at persons sentenced for crime in that way.

Let me depart from a negative finding; there are so few monsters in my country. I have never met one, nor have I written on the theme. The closest I have come to the topic was during a meeting in 'The American Society of Criminology' far back in time. Here, to my great astonishment, I found a session on "Monsters in crime". I attended. On the blackboard were listed several names. I can only remember one: Mr. Christie, the, at that time, famous mass-murderer from London. And one more memory: Queen Elizabeth was not named on the blackboard. Even though she – or her government – hanged Mr Evans for a killing they later found Christie had committed. But later her government also hanged Christie, so justice was restored.

Why are there so few monsters in my country? Perhaps I have not looked around with sufficient energy?

I have. As a very young student, I was approached by Johs Andenæs, professor of penal law, but at that time close to government, and Andreas Aulie, the general prosecutor. They had a problem. World War II was just over, Norway had been an occupied country for five years, now we were in the middle of a final cleaning process, those who had collaborated with the occupants or joined the Nazi party were all to be punished. Thousands were imprisoned. Twenty-five Norwegians were executed, the last one in 1948.

One problem intrigued the authorities. The Germans had created concentration camps for Yugoslavian partisans up in northern Norway; 2,717 arrived during the summer 1942. The following winter, 1,747 were killed by the guards or died from sickness, starvation or the extreme winter. Three hundred and sixty-three Norwegians served as guards, and 47 were sentenced after the war for killing or maltreatment of the prisoners.

I had long talks with nearly all of these 47 Norwegian guards and with a sample of guards who had been in the same situation without later being sentenced for having killed or maltreated prisoners. But I found no monsters, just ordinary people. I think I was able to explain some of the mechanisms that made killing possible, but concluded with a statement that I felt far from certain which group I would have ended up in myself, if I, at the age of 17, had been up there as a guard with gun in hand and surrounded with humans whom I did not see as such.

My preliminary results were published but politely ignored (Christie 1952). The extreme atrocities of concentration camps were for Germans to commit. If Norwegians took part, they had to be of a peculiar sort – Monsters. It was not until 20 years later, with a new generation of readers and with Milgram's (1965) results well known, that the full report was published and received with considerable interest (Christie 1972).

Since that time I have looked for monsters in and out of prisons, among drug users and importers, among people sentenced for violence as well as for disgusting sexual behaviour. Once I was supposed to meet a guaranteed monster. He had, for reasons that were difficult to understand, killed several people and put the blame on his girlfriend. For a long period he was the Swedish public enemy number one; a manhunt went on for weeks; a film on his life was made by a distinguished Swedish producer, and a monster was created. I went to see him and met a man like most men.[2] My search tells me that it seems possible to understand nearly everything without preconceptions that the offenders are outside the human family.

Are there absolutely no monsters around? May be I should not look so far away, at other people, but at myself and one or two colleagues. In a small country, those among us exposing controversial views become highly visible.[3] In Norway's public arena some of us might be seen as qualified for expulsion. In my case for arguing that people ought to get pensions rather than pain (Christie 1960); that one of the primary functions of schools – an arrangement close to prisons – is to keep children away from the lives of grown-ups (Christie 1971); that we ought to put *Limits to pain* (Christie 1981); and that drugs are "the useful enemy" (Christie and Bruun 1985). I have also been involved in actions of civil disobedience with some colleagues, resulting in a formal sentence, but this has not pushed us completely out of respectability.

What do I try to convey? That Norway is badly suited to the creation of monsters? We are too few? To a large extent, we know each other as persons with a wide variety of attributes. Those who killed in the concentration camps up in the north never really saw their victims as human beings. Those who did not kill, did. The man who made the film about the murderer had never talked to the supposed monster. Being visible in my home town, with friends and relatives of accepted calibre, a member of a faculty of law with close ties to power, it cannot be denied that at most I am OK, a bit naïve, but not necessarily evil. There is no fertile ground for my expulsion or creation as a monster.

Regarded as a person who is "okay ", if not quite reliable, I once functioned as a member of our Royal Commission on Penal Law – but only once, for a short period and for the consideration of a specific problem. The problem had to do with proposals for special measures for people seen as mentally deviant and potentially dangerous. I felt desperately alienated in the process, and ended up writing a 20-page dissenting vote, denouncing forensic psychiatry in general and its predictive ability in particular. The minister of justice at that time actually listened to me and shelved the majority proposal for new, special measures.[4] But relations with the majority of the Royal Commission had become somewhat tainted. They were the power-holders within our penal law establishment and I was never invited back to serve on the Commission. This experience has not filled my life with grief. On the contrary, in retrospect, I think it has been good, particularly for me and maybe also for certain aspects of criminology. My fate was to be forced to be an outsider but free to remain critical.

I got a sort of confirmation of this view of my persona through later contact with the same minister of justice. She is the best we have had in my lifetime – open, imaginative, with a sincere wish to create reform and, in addition, kind and pleasant as a person. Nonetheless, 20 years later, I have to confess a slight feeling of relief when a political shift brought her out of office. She asked me now and then for advice, and I had little to say, at least of the sort that might be useful for a politician. Youth crime was seen as a national problem. So, in my view, we ought to abolish youth and instead let children pass directly into adulthood, an idea that was not too helpful for the Labour Party. She also wanted to create a huge state committee for crime prevention. I felt as if this was observing a mosquito attacking an elephant and, again, that an explication of this view would not be particularly helpful, neither to the Minister I admired so much or to her party. Now and then the media asked for comment. She was the best minister ever. I did not want to hurt her. By not doing it, I was not free any more. Maybe it is not the worst of all solutions to preserve some distance between government and universities with room for critical thinking.

Back to monsters and the question, will Norway continue as an arena badly suited for the creation of monsters? In 1973, and in a new edition in 1982, I published a book called *How tightly knit a society?* (Christie 1982). The book's leading idea was explained initially through a diagram about crime against other people's honour, libel or defamation. My reasoning was simple: while everybody was concerned about the rise in crime, my concern was the rapid fall in this particular form of crime. My interpretation was not that people had become kinder to each other, that they took more care of other people's honour but the opposite. Honour was no longer so important.

Honour is important in a living society, one rich in social inter-action and social capital, which can be lost. In such a society honour might be so important that it leads to violence and killing. We live in the opposite situation, where honour is of limited importance; where there is little reason to raise complaints against defamation; where there is nothing to lose[5]. At the same time, such a society is one where individuals are more free, – for good and for bad.

Thus, the question arises, "How tightly knit a society? " How far, and with what sort of consequences, can our societies develop in a way that fosters the view that other people's opinions do not matter? How much can they develop a one-dimensional reward-system where the goal of economic success gains priority over alternative, old fashioned goals, moral fulfilment, artistic development, humanistic development, wisdom and so on? How much strain can a society absorb without losing its cohesive character?

A majority of Norwegians have decided, in two referendums, to remain outside the European Union. I agree wholeheartedly with my fellow Norwegians and my view is resonant of the criminological theory I advocate. To remain on the periphery, outside a gigantic organization with the purpose of increasing market forces, means at the same time attempting to preserve Norway as an independent country hoping to retain important civil qualities. But we are on the losing side. A belief in the beneficial effects of the market economy removes power from nation states. Even outside the EU, welfare states relegate welfare when money-movers can select the cheapest base for their operations – a country with a minimum of welfare.

The result is an increased difference between social segments. A common market leads to people with great differences in living standards living within a nation state. These days we experience a reappearance of the term "the dangerous classes". We also meet concepts and thinking from the military sector. No longer is there a war against poverty. The war is against crime, against drugs, with ghettos of the inner cities as the battleground. The military men are also mobilized, not only in words. The ministry of justice and the ministry of defence have joint meetings in Washington and elsewhere with the minister of justice conveying to the military people the message, "You won the war abroad. Now you must help us to win the war at home". Slowly, the military industry adapts their production to what is understood to be the needs of law and order.

In this setting we return to a fertile ground for monsters. The guards in concentration camps were no monsters but those who killed saw their prisoners that way. With the resurgence of the concept of "dangerous classes", combined with military technology, the ground is fertile for the reappearance of monsters – seen by those with power as dangerous non-humans.

We can observe how this trend develops, day by day and I have described some of it in *Crime control as industry* (Christie 1993). In 1992, when I wrote that book, the USA had 1,250,000 prisoners, or 505 per 100,000 inhabitants. In the second edition, written in 1994, they had 532 prisoners per 100,000 inhabitants. Writing this article in the end of 1996, I have calculated that they now have more than 1.7 million prisoners, or 650 per 100,000 inhabitants. Including those on probation and parole, they now have more than 5.6 million people under the control of the penal law system, which is more than 2 per cent of the population. Among males, there will be close to 4 per cent of the population, and among the younger half of males, at least 10 per cent will be under penal law control. In some states the proportion of young males in the control of the penal system will be close to 20 per cent, which comes close to a civil war, a civil war where the privileged have created their protected territories, using the state machinery or private police as their soldiers and prisons as places for internment. We are back to the great internment.

Are we also in Europe?

At the first Scottish Criminology Conference, held in Edinburgh in September 1996, James Q. Wilson presented a plenary about crime control. His message was clear and in harmony with his earlier writings. Increased use of imprisonment is the only practical solution to the USA's crime problem and Great Britain ought to follow the American example. However, as David Garland expressed in his prepared response to Wilson's paper:

> It is as if 19th century doctors, discovering that purging and leeches and surgery were much less effective than basic hygiene, decided that changing everyone's daily practices and building a new infrastructure of sewers would be too much trouble, too impractical, and so decided to stick to the old

medicine, even if mortality rates and iatrogenic diseases were embarrassingly high.

Wilson's ideas hold considerable sway in Anglo–American societies but there are also some signs of countervailing forces. The extreme growth in the number of intellectuals in industrialized societies might open the way for a measure of protection against the consequences of the market economy and the accompanying dangers of ending up in conditions close to civil war. The growth in the number of students will probably create a huge academic surplus. Surplus in the sense that they will not all get a paid job where their education is of relevance to their employment. They might in the future end up as members of a highly educated proletarian class, with income from social security, or, in the best case, from a basic minimum wage for all. In this situation they will nevertheless remain as a category particularly trained for cultural activities. Intellectuals, artists and old fashioned craftsmen, probably what is called "artisans" by the English, have one activity in common – they build. They build with music, clay, paint, figures or words. Absorbed in their métier, their activity will often be transformed from labour to work, or in the German version, *Werk*, that final goal for creation. When that happens the market economy loses its totalitarian reign. Human beings find other reasons than money for labour, and wealth ceases as the symbol of fulfilment of life.

Life in smaller societies might strengthen these developments. For example, several regions in Europe struggle for independence, and develop a type of counter culture. To be a Basque, a Corsican, a Sicilian or a member of the Sami-community in the north of Scandinavia might foster identities outweighing the market value of an individual. Several religious movements might have the same function. Identity becomes established as an alternative to money.

None of this is to imply that these or any other small scale societies represent a sort of paradise. They might be terrible, with strict standards, extreme surveillance, all knowing all about all, modern men and women escaping into solitude and loneliness with a sigh of relief. We nevertheless also know that some of them have extraordinary qualities, qualities we have to analyse and understand.

Living in small regions, or small national states, certainly influences the type of intellectual work carried out within them. In small societies, several things happen. First, it is not so easy to shy away from taking part in the general cultural and political debate about how to run the country. It is like living in a small cottage. There are no janitors. We have to mend damage ourselves and people become more active.

Small nations tend to have a very large number of newspapers, which are read! Iceland is at the top of Europe in this respect. Her population is concerned, encouraging social scientists to write and talk so that everybody can follow discussion. In addition we do not need to write for national colleagues. They are so few, we can talk when we occasionally meet.

Since we are so few, we are also tempted to cover relatively large areas, which means that specialization is discouraged. Again, this has consequences for the style of writing practised. It is a deviant style when compared to the mainstream Anglo–American tradition. This point was actually illustrated in discussions around this very essay. My editors were indeed kind, positive and encouraging as to the major content, but were also of the opinion that it read more like a sketch than a fully worked-up paper. They appreciated that I discussed all my points more fully and hoped that "you would widen out from your own writings to consider where your work sits in relation to other criminologists. You have 8,000 words as a limit".

To me, 8,000 words were not a limit but a treat. I live in an academic setting with emphasis on an essayistic tradition, essays in the original meaning of being attempts – attempts to combine a variety of insights and perspectives. This is probably a more natural form in societies where a small number of people have to cover large fields, contrasting with the situation in societies where a large number of social scientists within each speciality makes for a greater tendency to turn every stone, including the totality of those already turned by colleagues. Happily, the editors let me get away with my national peculiarities, which means acceptance of the value of essays written for a general audience. For years my advice to myself, students and colleagues has been to write with your favourite aunt in mind. Favourite aunts are willing to give the ideas a try, but do not finish reading if points are mystified in scientific jargon.

The effect of all this has been increased by an accidental factor in my life. It has so happened that I often lecture to people seen by others as dumb, retarded or feeble-minded. I call them extra-ordinary, and the experience has helped to strengthen a deep conviction that I have nothing of importance to say that cannot be understood by most people (Christie 1989).

These experiences also have consequences in situations where it is necessary to express ideas in other people's language. This can be done in two ways, through the academic language of a particular country or in my native way, inspired by aunts and extraordinary people. Of course I cling to the last alternative, trying to keep the melody of my Norwegian and the simplicity inherent in my limited vocabulary. Favourite aunts, extraordinary people and linguistic handicaps force me down to basics. This is dangerous, it is not possible to hide behind elegance and form. Feeling safe in my little sanctuary, I can afford to take that risk.

Clearly, this wish to take part in the general debate in a small country, and particularly to communicate with all sorts of people, is far from unproblematic. The choice of research themes will not so easily be determined by the agenda presented in the international literature (even if I must confess to a considerable amount of fatigue browsing some of the international journals). Instead the choice will be influenced by what is seen as important by a broad segment within the national system. The researcher might thus lose connection with relevant theories. On the other hand, small scale societies make it natural to look for totalities, which leads the researcher back to variables of a general, theoretical nature.

Another problem with small-scale societies is once more the danger in ending up too close to power. Norway is a hawk on drug policy. Our extreme restrictions on methadone makes people suffer and die. With colleagues, I take part in attempts to convince the Minister of Social Affairs that she has to change this policy. With this activity, I am back to the old danger of co-optation. We have to relate to power, be close but not too close. Close because we live here, meet people in severe trouble, in need of help or living in conditions so bad that it is a moral obligation to strive for change. But we must not be so close as to loose the ability to look at the phenomena as outsiders, with the joy and freshness of ethnographers or social anthropologists. Distant and close.

In the old days the courts had a jester – not the worst position for observation – offering insight and some influence. Today, some of these activities might be seen as cared for by cultural commentators, impractical women and men of letters. The criminology I like is one carried out from an impossible position in the middle of a triangle between government, human misery and academic demands. My identity is one of a cultural worker, one close to other people of letters. We know so little that government is willing or able to use. At the same time we see so much misery that we have to act. We need to conceptualize our insights and give them forms that enable us to take part in great intellectual dialogues. This is not done out of any hope for progress. I do not believe in any general development towards general higher social forms or states. My life has been more a number of attempts to understand where we are and who we are, combined with a struggle for decency within these forms.

Many authors stick to the same theme during most of their lifetime; I do also. I commenced my scientific life with a deficit in monsters. I am now enlarging on that topic in essays where one of the major propositions is that crime does not exist (Christie 1996a, b). Again, the theme is simple. In the beginning there were acts. Then followed discussions on their qualities. Some acts are seen as terrible, according to most standards in most societies, certainly according to my own. Terrible acts, however, can be met in various ways. In certain situations they are given the meaning of crime, and action seen as crime control is initiated. In other situations the same unwanted acts are again seen as terrible, but suited to sanctions such as social distance, expulsion, ridicule or demands for compensation. One of the challenges for criminology is to analyse the social conditions giving unwanted acts their particular meaning. In this activity, criminology might be able to give advice on how to find, preserve and nurture those social conditions which work against recent trends of seeing so many unwanted acts as crime in need of penal action. Instead we could open the way for alternative forms of perception and alternative ways of control. Doing this, criminology might come to play an important role in the defence of civil society.

Notes

1 Thanks to the editors and to Stan Cohen, Randi Ervik, Katja Franko, Hedda Giertsen and Cecilie Høigård for stimulating comments.

2 He was a Finn of Sami descent, particularly well suited as raw material for images of extreme deviance. It is one of my many cases of omission that I have not written down the life-story of this man.

3 It is particularly Cecilie Høigård and Thomas Mathiesen I have in mind, both social scientists within the faculty of law, University of Oslo.

4 Last year a new proposal for special measures – new, but with essentially the old content – was launched and was accepted by both minister and Parliament.

5 These ideas are, of course, close to Braithwaite's (1987a) on shame. But we could not know and quote from my text. My ideas on honour were safely hidden in a Norwegian/Danish edition, it was not until 1980 I wrote my books in English (and thereafter rewrote them in Norwegian).

CHAPTER 8

From criminology to anthropology? Identity, morality and normality in the social construction of deviance

Richard Jenkins

...the concept "punishment" possesses in fact not one meaning but a whole synthesis of meanings ...Punishment as a means of rendering harmless, of preventing further harm ... as recompense to the injured party for the harm done ...as the isolation of a disturbance of equilibrium ...as a means of inspiring fear of those who determine and execute the punishment ... as the expulsion of a degenerate element ...as a festival ...as the making of a memory, whether for him who suffers the punishment – so-called "improvement" – or for those who witness its execution ...as a compromise with revenge ...This list is certainly not complete; it is clear that punishment is overdetermined by utilities of all kinds.

Friedrich Nietzsche 1887 (1989: 80–81)

This chapter distils a series of debates which I had with myself, and with successive groups of undergraduate students, while I was teaching in the department of sociology and anthropology at the University of Wales, Swansea.[1] The catalyst that precipitated these thoughts was the departure in the mid-1980s of the colleague who had been teaching "crime and deviance" in the department. I had a long-standing interest in deviance, as a consequence of research that I had done on historical witchcraft in Ireland (Jenkins 1977) and working-class youth and the transition to adulthood (1982, 1983). I was also teaching the course – focusing primarily on the early modern European witchcraft persecutions – that was administratively linked to the crime and deviance course. So, I ended up teaching both.

The ideas in this chapter, then, evolved in an immediate sense out of my desire to produce courses – one on witchcraft, one on deviance and social control – that were as integrated as possible, conceptually, and out of the need to teach about deviance in such a way as to speak successfully to students of both social anthropology and sociology. In other words, I wanted to offer a properly interdisciplinary view on the social construction of deviance. If the evidence of student coursework was anything to go by, I only ever partially achieved that ambition. However, the attempt inspired me to bring to bear on the analysis of crime and deviance a range of social anthropological arguments and points of view which had hitherto been little exploited in that context. The *specific* emphasis, upon discourses of identity, morality and normality, was to a considerable extent the consequence of the link with the witchcraft course, where these issues were conspicuous and pressing. Therefore, if nothing else, this chapter will, I hope, testify to the continuing centrality of teaching to the intellectual enterprises that we know as the social sciences.

There is also a less easily summarized, and less immediate, genealogy for the ideas which I present in this chapter (see also Jenkins 1996, 1997). Although my undergraduate and postgraduate education was in social anthropology, I was fortunate in that my teachers – particularly John Blacking, Milan Stuchlik and Jack Goody – were no respecters of disciplinary boundaries. Serendipity played its part too; I can still remember the thrill of recognition in picking up, in the student's union second-hand book shop at the Queen's University of Belfast, Howard Becker's *Outsiders* (1963). It was immediately clear to me that this stuff was relevant to anthropology. The subsequent path that my academic career took in the SSRC Research Unit on Ethnic Relations and the Department at Swansea further reinforced this interdisciplinarity; to the extent that the question of my disciplinary identity – whether sociology or social anthropology – is something that interests other people more than it does me. It has become second nature for me to seek answers to the questions thrown up by one field in the other. As, I hope, in the discussion that follows.

What is to be done about criminology?

Although it was important in the development of social theory in the 1950s and 1960s, the sociology of deviance has become something of a backwater, dominated these days by the narrow concerns of criminology. The emergence of specialist sociologies of sexuality, youth, health and illness (particularly with respect to mental illness), and social control (inspired by Foucault), has been at the expense of the sociological study of deviance. The scholastic demands of increasing disciplinary specialization mean that few general social theorists regard deviance as one of the areas with which they should be concerned. Where there has been theoretical development – for example, in the articulation of a feminist critique (Smart 1976; Morris 1987) – it has focused on criminology. There has also been a political shift, from radical to applied criminology; its practitioners seem largely content to tread theoretical water, their attention concentrated upon policy-related empirical research (Rock 1988). The project of a wide-ranging sociology of deviance is currently neglected, if not abandoned altogether. The situation is sufficiently desperate to have provoked a book-length "obituary" (Sumner 1994).

However, a broad approach is not without its problems. It is a commonplace of introductory sociology courses that deviance is a more general phenomenon than crime. But while crime is conveniently defined as practices which are legally categorized in any social context as criminal, defining deviance is nothing like as straightforward. Deviance, as an analytical and as a commonsensical notion, conflates and confuses a number of distinct themes. The sociology of deviance, in reflection of this underlying conceptual difficulty, encompasses research into an enormous range of social phenomena: disabilities, organized crime, witchcraft persecutions, sado-masochism, mad scientists, mad people in general, child abuse, youth lifestyles, and so on in a very long list (see Becker 1964; Ben-Yahuda 1985; Bryant 1990; Freilich et al. 1991).

Sociological discourse about deviance is unified by the principle that deviance is, in some sense, the violation of a norm. That norm may be supplied by common sense, by the law, by psychological or medical diagnosis, or, indeed, by the sociologist. Its heterogeneous sources aside, the word *norm* masks a diversity of yardsticks, from the moral to the statistical. Such a broad and poorly-specified concept – which is as definitively "overdetermined", *pace* Nietzsche, as a concept could be – may be a useful "sensitising notion" (Downes and Rock 1988: 187–8), but if the sociology of deviance, rather than the sociology of crime, is to move beyond its present theoretical impasse, in which little of novelty or note has appeared since the wave of work in the fifties and sixties inspired by symbolic interactionism and phenomenology, some conceptual clarification is needed.

Conceptual clarification is not all that is required. There may be a need to *justify* the retention of the sociology of deviance, as a distinct subfield of the discipline. Looked at dispassionately, should we persist in an endeavour that appears to have lost its way – if not to be in total disarray, that has in some important respects been swallowed or annexed by another institutional domain in the shape of criminology, the subject matter of which may not actually be clear, and that at best defines its field of interest as a residual category?

There are, however, convincing reasons for persisting. Regardless of the opinions of sociologists, lay people recognize and are intensely interested in something called *deviance* – or whatever its local version might be – and that recognition and interest is powerfully constitutive of the social world. This seems to hold good in all local and cultural settings (and regardless of the presence or absence of a notion of *crime*). The sociology of deviance is not, therefore, hemmed in by the local institutional frameworks of criminal law: it is, potentially at least, a more universalizing discourse. It may, if you like, be about issues that are bigger than the often parochial, typically policy-related, concerns of criminology. What is more, because all cultures and localities offer the researcher some common sense notions of deviance, and because these are important to everyday interaction and the social construction of identity and selfhood – a point which only requires passing reference to Goffman for its justification – the study of deviance is among the most strategic of fields for meta-disciplinary theory building, able to draw upon social anthropology, social psychology and sociology. As this chapter seeks to demonstrate, in this respect we have not yet exhausted the possibilities for theorizing the social

136

construction of deviance. As in the past, theoretical developments with respect to deviance in general are likely to be consequential for the theorization of crime in particular; this is particularly true if, with due respect to the general thrust of this volume, the social theory of criminology is as much in the doldrums as the sociology of deviance.

Different kinds of deviance

The notion of deviance *per se* may not – àpropos norms – be the best starting point in the quest for clarification. As a social anthropologist, my starting point for the meta-disciplinary approach proposed above is – particularly with an eye on the relativities of cultural variation – to ask, "deviant with respect to *what*?" Within which frameworks of judgement and comparison is it possible to classify persons and behaviour as deviant? Bearing in mind the variety of uses to which the notion is put, there are arguably at least three such paradigms of deviance: *social identity, morality* and *normality*. Although conceptually distinct, these often become entangled in each other because of their systematic interrelationship in the social construction of categories of deviance.

Among other things, social identity refers to how an "X" can be expected to behave and what an actor would have to do in order to claim successfully to be an "X". It is a question of how we see ourselves and how others see us. Models of social identity contribute to our anticipation of the future behaviour of others. Our expectations of others, in particular those about whom we have limited information, often depend upon what we perceive their identity to be, in terms of gender, ethnicity, age category, occupation or whatever. Social identity thus mitigates interactional uncertainty. However, our expectations in this respect do not necessarily derive from knowledge based in experience. Stereotypes are too common in the social construction of identity, as is a time lag between changes in behaviour and any concomitant changes in perceptions, for us to imagine identity as anything other than a useful fiction, albeit a very consequential fiction. Social identity is imagined but not imaginary (Jenkins 1996).

Morality is the normative and evaluative ordering of the world which is codified – insofar as morality is as systematic as that word may suggest – in culture. Concerned in the first instance with the distinction between good and evil, morality is prescriptive of behaviour, rather than descriptive; it is about what ought to be the case than what actually is. Morality and social identity interact, of course. Social identity often – or at least ideally – entails adherence to appropriate moral principles (loyalty to which may, in turn, contribute to the attribution or espousal of identity). Thus moral norms are frequently specific to, or implicated in, particular identities; social identity is both prescriptive and descriptive.

Should we, therefore, seek to disentangle morality and identity? There are several reasons for doing so. Some social identities, for example, are defined as deviant without any moral judgement being entailed: they may be spoiled, otherwise imperfect or simply out-of-the-ordinary, but not bad or evil. Similarly, a person may be incompetent or inappropriate in an identity, without necessarily attracting moral evaluation. And some deviance – invention, for example – may be morally positively evaluated by others.

Both description and prescription imply a degree of predictability; the first describes how things can reasonably be expected to be, the second seeks to construct the future in a particular way. Uncertainty about future behaviour is one criterion of deviance. Although madness, for example, is defined, in part, by its exemption from moral judgement on the grounds of diminished responsibility, another element in its definition is unpredictability of a particular severity. That severity is, in part at least, assessed by reference to the gulf between the expectations attached to the person's other or previous identities and their new behaviour.

Social identity and morality have always been important in human social life. The notion of normality, however, is modern. The statistically normal, socially, is that range of behaviour which is held to occur within a predictable degree of greatest frequency, as mapped, for example, by the bell-shaped curve of normal distribution. The boundary between that which the normal and that which is not is arbitrary. Again, predictability is important. The social project which informed the nineteenth-century definition of the normal distribution has been characterized as the "taming of chance" (Hacking 1990). The underlying theme is social control;

population statistics are collected and analysed in order to forecast social trends, a vital contribution to governmental planning. The normal distribution, embodied in statistically-validated psychometric tests, also underpins predictive instruments for the individual diagnosis of deficiency and excellence with respect to capacities which are valued in industrial societies: intelligence, communicative competence, social skills, particular aptitudes (Cohen, S. 1985: 183–96; Hanson 1993). Individuals are categorized under the aegis of the test's legitimate authority, and this identification influences the allocation of a range of resources and penalties – social control, again.

The recognition of the common, and therefore predictable, behaviour patterns of others has always been part of the construction of social identity. In antiquity literacy and numeracy began to make possible the objective, decontextualized comparison which is a prerequisite for the conceptualization of the normal. We can discern ancestors of modern notions of normality in classical concepts such as the Pythagorean golden mean. However, it was post-Enlightenment mathematics that established the concept of statistical normality and its parameters. Over the last century and a half or so, the interaction of a statistical model of the social world with notions of deviance based in morality and identity has produced a new scientifically-legitimated, quantitative model of normality. In a democratizing social shift of emphasis towards the celebration of the average, the impulse favouring normality has become more demanding than conformist morality and more explicit than everyday criteria of social identity. The meaning and definition of right and wrong is no longer to be found either in divine ordination or the entailments of group membership. Now it may also be discovered objectively, expressed in the laws of biology or social structure.

The degree to which a discourse about deviance-in-the-abstract has become possible at all is eloquent tribute to the paradigmatic domination of the scientifically rigorous model of normality in twentieth-century Western consciousness. Part of the rationalization of modernity, it both rivals and conspires with morality:

One can ...use the word "normal" to say how things are, but also to say how they ought to be. The magic of the word is that we can use it to do both things at once. The norm may be what is usual or typical, yet our most powerful ethical constraints are also called norms. (Hacking 1990:163)

But if the analytical conceptualization of deviance owes its existence to the notion of normality, therein also lie the roots of the definitional confusion which the present discussion is attempting to clarify.

In addition to its scientific authority, normality has thus assumed some of the legitimacy deriving from morality and identity. This is in part a result of the interaction between the three which is a recurrent aspect of the modern world. Social states and conditions of one sort or another are increasingly labelled as normal (or not). This authoritative diagnosis of the subnormal, the abnormal and the better-than-normal has produced a range of unforgivingly solid social identities – of which mentally handicapped, homosexual and above average intelligence are, respectively, examples – which simply did not, as we know them today, exist in earlier epochs.

My argument, then, is that there are three different thematic counterpoints in the social orchestration of deviance: social identity, morality and normality. Each theme is available to speakers and to audiences whenever the notion is invoked. There are three different meanings, but, in deviance, only one enormously powerful word.

Social identity

Social identity is the integrating concept of this discussion because it emphasizes the framework of membership within which deviance becomes possible. Two other important facets of social identity, for the purposes of this discussion, are first, that it necessarily involves processes of social inclusion and exclusion, but that, second, these processes work across open rather than closed boundaries, osmotic continua of *us* and *them*.

What else is meant by social identity? The concept refers to the processes through which individuals and groups distinguish them-selves as different *from* others and similar *to* others. One of the most important anthropological insights in this respect is that social identity is frequently situationally defined, variable and, to some extent, negotiable (Barth 1969; Jenkins 1996). Some identities – for example, primary identities which are acquired during very early socialization, or those which are definitively embodied, such as race, disability or gender – are, however, less malleable than others. Social identities are, what is more, typically hierarchically structured from the collectively general to the individually particular, with differing degrees of relative social consequence or weight. There is the possibility, for any individual, of conflict between identities within this hierarchy. Although social identity always depends upon their mutual interaction, it is important analytically to distinguish differences of emphasis between *internally-defined* identities, claimed by the individual or by group members themselves, and *externally-defined* identities, imposed or otherwise projected by others onto an individual or social category (Jenkins 1994, 1996). Many deviant identities, at least in the first instance, are externally defined.

Fredrik Barth argues that social boundaries persist despite interaction – and the occasional flow of personnel – across them. Self-identification by actors themselves is important, as is their categorization by others; the existence of social groups depends upon the practical accomplishment, on the inside and the outside, of boundary maintenance, involving the ongoing use and review of criteria of group membership and the rules or principles governing interaction across the boundary. These criteria, rules and principles can be implicit or explicit. Building in part upon Barth, Anthony Cohen emphasizes the *symbolic* power of notions of communality and group membership (Cohen, A.P. 1985), arguing that the symbolization of social boundaries permits a degree of unity to co-exist with social diversity. The symbolized group is a house within which there are many mansions. Another appropriate metaphor might be that of an umbrella under which diversity can shelter. This avoids the temptation to conceptualize community life, and the existence of communities themselves, as predicated upon normative or, indeed, cognitive consensus. Both Barth and Cohen agree, however, that community membership is made and remade during interaction; communal identity must be validated (or not) by significant others.

Interaction as the context within which social membership is achieved, emphasizes the importance of *conformity* (as opposed to consensus). The social construction of conformity is also an aspect of the attempt to render interaction predictable. Social psychology suggests (Aronson 1991: 12–55) that two goals inspire conformism: the desire to be correct and the desire to remain in the good graces of others. The first has most affect on private judgements, the second on public behaviour, but each derives from primary socialization, and each is emotionally rooted in the desire to *belong*. External factors which shape conformist goal orientations vary by culture, social situation and individual biography. Nonconformity may – only apparently paradoxically – have fewer costs for those whose group membership is secure; insecure membership may be a potent pressure in the direction of conformity (although one would expect there to be a point of marginality beyond which this is no longer true). This is reminiscent of Cohen's argument about the symbolic power of boundaries to license or accommodate a degree of dissensus within them.

There is, of course, more to conformity than the pursuit of goals. Aronson specifies a number of other reasons for conformity. *Compliance* results from compulsion. It may only be weak conformity, and may not survive the relaxation of the coercion, but it is significant. *Identification* depends upon affect and attraction, in intimate dyadic relationships and in collective or public contexts. Identification, of course, is arguably related to the desire to stay in the good graces of others. Finally, *internalization*, is an outcome of socialization, calculation and rationalization; conformity is identified as the most sensible response to the demands of the situation. Sorting out internalization from the desire to be correct is not straightforward, however. Local notions of what counts as correct are central to both; in both the motivation to be right (or, at least, not wrong) is taken for granted. What is more, the rational thing to do in many situations may be to stay in the good graces of others. Compulsion aside, therefore, the distinction between goal-oriented and non goal-oriented conformity is, at best, analytical.

Weber's famous discussion of domination (1978: 53–4, 212–301), contains some interestingly parallel observations. Conformity can be understood as product, object and expression of domination. Power, the domination of others through coercion, is the pursuit of compliance. Power, however, has a more routine and more efficient alternative: *authority* is legitimate domination, the obedience of those who accept its demands as justified (Smith, M.G. 1960: 15–33). Identification and internalization can both be recognized within Weber's categorization of legitimate domination: the first is the basis of charismatic authority, the second of either legal or traditional authority.

Coming back to predictability, social psychology also suggests that there is likely to be a relationship between conformity and uncertainty. If one is unsure of the rules or norms in any situation, the behaviour of others is frequently the single most important source of information about the situationally appropriate thing to do, and imitation produces conformity. This is of major significance for the way in which children acquire cultural knowledge, but it remains important throughout adult life.

From a different point of view, Mary Douglas suggests that fears of ritual pollution and supernatural danger, and protective measures against them, reinforce other social factors encouraging conformity (Douglas, M.L. 1966). The emphasis is upon symbolic classification, upon boundaries between different membership roles within groups, between appropriate and inappropriate behaviour, between dirt and cleanliness, etc. "Dirt", she argues, "is the by-product of a systematic ordering and classification of matter"(ibid: 48). For the sociologist of deviance this quotation should ring interesting bells. It can be paraphrased thus: deviance is the by-product of a systematic ordering and classification of behaviour and persons. It is an analogue of the canonical first principle of the labelling perspective: "social groups create deviance by making the rules whose infraction constitutes deviance" (Becker 1963: 9).

Social life is unimaginable without the classificatory systems provided in culture; without them we simply could not know anything, or anybody or even ourselves. Every social group has characteristic classificatory systems (even if only modestly characteristic); some participation in them is a criterion of group membership. Among other things, classification focuses attention on boundaries: of the group, of acceptable behaviour, of purity, of humanity, of whatever. Stereotyping, prejudice and attribution are important aspects of classification (Aronson 1991: 12–55; Tajfel 1981). Stereotyping is the labelling and classification of social collectivities, albeit in a partial fashion; it simplifies information inputs and outputs about complex situations, distilling the complex to the simple. It can be understood as an extreme example of routine classificatory processes and broadly similar to processes of typification which – concerned as they are with predictability – are central to habituation and institutionalization (Berger and Luckmann 1967: 74–5)

However, stereotyping is not just a functional matter of information management. Boundary maintenance and symbolization, harking back to Barth and Cohen, must also be taken into account. It is in the nature of stereotypes – in their compression of information, in their part-for-whole quality, in their dramatic exaggeration – that they will be powerfully symbolic:

> symbols exhibit the properties of *condensation, unification of disparate referents,* and *polarisation of meaning.* A single symbol, in fact, represents many things at the same time: it is multi-vocal, not uni-vocal (Turner, V.W. 1974: 48).

Because of their dramatizing and polarizing symbolic properties, stereotypical depictions of – and by – people on either side of a social boundary are likely to demarcate its contours with (illusory) precision.

Attribution is the attempt to understand others – especially their motivations – by inference from the limited data provided by their verbal and non-verbal behaviour. It is also at work in stereotyping. Attribution is a strategy for understanding and rendering more predictable the social world. We all, all of the time, need to explain and anticipate what other people are doing. In order to do so, we need, much of the time, to go beyond the information which is available to us. The routine ambiguity and uncertainty of such situations leads, Aronson suggests, to frequent recourse to stereotypical attributions. It is probably not coincidental, therefore, that anomaly and ambiguity often attract a symbolic load or marker (Douglas, D. 1966: 41–53). Boundaries and borders are often unclear or ambiguous, hence the need to map them with altogether imaginary precision.

To sum up, although group membership is delineated in collective classification and boundary maintenance, the practices of individuals are also important. Group membership, as a practical accomplishment, demands at least a degree of behavioural conformity. This does not, however, mean the existence of a consensus: the symbolization of group boundaries (the "umbrella"), the distinction between private judgements and public behaviour, and the different ways in which domination can be said to work, all suggest that consensual values are unnecessary for shared social identity to exist.

This suggests that marginal membership need not imply normative dissensus. Nor need deviance. Nor, to push the point further, need deviance imply either marginality or dissensus. At the boundaries of a group, frameworks of predictability falter; there may be ambiguity not only about criteria of membership – who is in and who is not – but also about what counts as appropriate behaviour. Group boundaries, the negotiated practical sense of us and them, may, therefore, be generated in and by uncertainty, emerging as an ordering response to the relative unpredictability of others. In fact, strong pressures encouraging conformity – and severe penalties attaching to deviance – may not only be experienced by, but also *produced* by, those whose membership or social identity is most insecure. Tolerance may not be an affordable luxury. Powerful signals about conformity and deviance, relating to group membership and boundaries, can be expressed symbolically, in stereotypes of insiders and outsiders. For those on the edges of membership, the price of belonging may be some suppression of their own ambiguity (and that of others), and the minor tyranny of the predictability demanded by others. The less securely an individual belongs, or the more he or she wants or needs to, the higher that price is likely to be.

Morality

With some notable exceptions (see Douglas, J.R. 1970), recent sociology has not been very interested in the social construction of moral categories; in as much as its field of concern is predetermined by the law, criminology can afford to take them for granted, if not ignore them altogether. Anthropology has a greater tradition of interest in morality, focusing in particular on concepts of *evil* (Parkin 1985). This emphasis may reflect the fact that *good* is a more elusive concept than evil: while we do not necessarily expect our fellows to exhibit the former, we hope not to encounter the latter too often. The boundaries beyond which lie wickedness and evil are – like "red for danger" road signs – generally better marked symbolically than those which differentiate the mundane from the virtuous. However, applying the general cartography of evil to specific cases is frequently an uncertain enterprise; hence another source of the symbolization of the maleficent, and hence too the fact that we are often quicker to judge the bad than to praise the good.

The greater visibility of evil – and, indeed, its mystery – is commonly held to reflect the general human experience of life as a vale of tears: "Human beings …face the *existential* problem of whether and how a life laced with suffering and punctuated by death can have any positive meaning" (Adams and Adams 1990: 1).

The premier salience of evil in the moral construction of the social world is probably also, however, bound up with the suspicion that the costs attached to ignoring evil are greater than those attendant upon a neglect of the good. This principle may explain the socio-logical preoccupation with deviance rather than its opposite, but it may also explain two further, and related, facets of the social construction of good and evil. First, moral vigilance is preventative, concerned with what people might do in addition to what they have already done. Second, a preventative or predictive interest in wickedness may produce a concern with evil *thoughts* as well as evil *deeds*.

Notions of evil appear, therefore, to be rooted in a number of different aspects of the human predicament. It must also be remembered that they are relative, varying between cultures and epochs. Correspondingly, they attract a variety of explanations. The most conventional, perhaps, is that the notion of evil serves to explain misfortune and unhappiness. There is doubtless a large grain of truth in this.

However, some things – an example is homosexuality – arguably only become a misfortune or a cause of unhappiness *because* they are labelled an evil. The conventional wisdom that the notion of evil explains misfortune is further modified by Pocock's suggestion that it reflects the human disposition to create ideals against which life cannot possibly measure (Pocock 1985). Of necessity things must go wrong, because we expect too much, particularly, perhaps, of other people. Attribution theory in social psychology offers related ideas

(Aronson 1991: 12–55). There appears, for example, to be a tendency for actors to attribute their own errors to situational factors, but those made by others to their individual shortcomings. Notions of evil, viewed in this light, permit the externalization of responsibility for our problems onto other people. Aronson argues further that "blaming the victim" reflects a human need to believe that the world is fair (i.e. predictably ordered in its outcomes by moral principles). Therefore, if people fail it must be their own fault, an interpretation which resonates with Pocock's point about unrealistically high expectations.

Not everyone, however, accepts the human ubiquity of some of these needs and predicaments. For example, *contra* conventional wisdom, Mary Douglas argues that, "Pain and injustice do not pose problems, social or religious, for everyone" (1973: 136). For her, the problem of evil only becomes significant where social control is strong:

> For each distinct type of social environment ...there is its necessary manner of justifying coercion. Through the classifications used, the furniture of the universe is turned into an armoury of control. In each social system human suffering is explained in a way that reinforces the controls. To see how evil is understood, we must see classification and personal pressure ...working together (ibid.).

Deviance, once again, is the product of social control. In modern states, increasing social and institutional complexity, pluralism and heterogeneity are likely to be associated with an expansion in the reach, scope and inflexibility of formal social control, as well as an increasingly specialized classificatory division of labour. Following Douglas, and in general agreement with Foucault (Foucault 1979; see also Cohen, S. 1985), these trends may lead to increasingly authoritative and authoritarian moral categorizations. However, the areas of social life which are specifically controlled through the mobilization of criteria of morality – rather than identity or normality – may actually (and only apparently paradoxically) contract with the advent of modernity. Moral categories and boundaries are likely to become harder and less permeable as their field of relevance declines.

Just as hygiene creates dirt, so moral classification produces notions of evil as well as standards of virtue. To say this is to revisit – with perhaps a detour via the labelling perspective *en route* – a set of time-hallowed ideas with their social science roots in Durkheim. However, within the boundaries of the everyday, between the symbolically-charged poles of negative and positive, is a field of uncertainty. Not everything which attracts moral disapproval is evil: some things are merely bad, unkind or just naughty. Others are controversial in their moral evaluation and others again attract little or no moral attention. As a consequence, moral categories, their limits and their application are potential nodes of struggle and social conflict.

Although uncertainty is likely to proliferate with social change, and with the increasing scale and heterogeneity of the social arenas which offer us frameworks for judgement in modern society, there are no grounds for thinking that it is anything other than a routine dimension of all social life. Bearing in mind the uneasy relationship between normative rules and what people actually do (Holy and Stuchlik 1983: 20–44), and the improvizatory character of social interaction (Bourdieu 1990), this is no more than one would expect. There is a limit to the degree to which morality can *determine* practice, a limit beyond which behaviour is informed by a complex calculus of uncertainty, self-interest, constraint and the trajectories of possibility.

Returning to the relationship between identity and morality, how do questions of belonging and of evil fit together? For Barth, group membership implies that an individual should be recognized by others as a particular kind of person. Group identity, therefore, implies a claim to be judged – and to judge oneself – by the moral standards which apply to that identity (Barth 1969: 14). Thus morality is relative, embedded within social identity. It is also em-bedded within social relationships of inclusion and exclusion (witness the good behaviour which stems from the desire to be well-thought of or accepted). On the one hand, there is *belief* the internalization of the canons of moral right and wrong which are entailed by a particular belonging. On the other, there is *bad faith*, instrumental conformity in order to belong. In between there is a continuum of combinations of the two which are difficult to disentangle.

Douglas is right, however, to argue that the power of group norms – regardless, I suspect, of whether we are talking about good or bad faith – is variable. Where group membership criteria are at their most compelling there also are models of good and evil likely to be most imperative. This suggests what comparative ethnography and history confirm: some identities are more tightly structured or demanding, and some classificatory systems more ordered, than others. Some social settings are characterized by more monitoring of morality and deviance than others.

These arguments offer a mild corrective to the Durkheimian view – offered by Anthony Cohen, for example (1985: 58–69) – that the symbolization of deviance, typically in ritual, reinforces the cultural mainstream and the boundaries of group identity. Douglas is correct to point out the variability with which this process operates. However, the general argument is clearly right. Ritual does simultaneously symbolize moral boundaries and group boundaries, and the importance of that symbolization in fostering belief and dramatizing the social sanctions which attach to deviance cannot be ignored. Further, if the behavioural criteria of group membership are more demanding for those who are marginal, then ritualized stereotypes of good and evil are likely to be most dramatic at the boundary.

Morality is necessarily double-edged. It offers some defence against the evil of others, but only at the expense of some surrender of self-determination, some submission to control by others. Each is necessarily implicated in the other (cf. Thompson 1975: 258–69). One dramatic expression of these themes is the figure of the outlaw, banished beyond the moral boundaries of society, from whom the protection of morality and law *and* the constraints of group membership are simultaneously withdrawn. The revealing paradox of the outlaw genre of folk tales, however, is that in myth the outlaw often appears as the symbol of true membership, custodian of the authentic values of the group. In the absence of King Richard, Robin Hood was the true guardian and leader of Merry England, the Sheriff of Nottingham the real alien. A better dramatization of the relationship between group identity and morality is difficult to imagine.

RICHARD JENKINS

Normality

The commonsensical, philosophical and theological discourses that frame our thinking about identity and morality have long histories. Normality, however, is not only a recent notion, but it is still relatively taken-for-granted. This may be – and only apparently paradoxically – because, in one sense, there is nothing new about normality. Culture, if it is nothing else, is a classificatory compendium of the routine. People have always had a reasonable idea of the difference between the usual and the unusual, the expected and the unexpected, the predictable and the unpredictable, and this has always been important in the constitution of social identities. However, this common sense was and is – because it remains important – an implicit, unelaborated model of normality, which is anchored in the specifics of particular situations and things.

The modern, statistical understanding of normality differs from this traditional concept in two respects. First, it is explicitly defined, according to specified criteria of frequency and distribution. Second, it is a general model of abstract normality, applicable to, but independent of, substantive particulars. Although the fine theoretical points of this explicit model of normality have not penetrated everyday discourse, the traditional implicit understanding of predictable routine has been substantially supplemented and modified by the conceptual and institutional power of normality.

The word and the idea are supported by the power and authority of science. The emerging statistical model of normality grew in significance with the development during the nineteenth century, in Europe and North America in particular, of philosophies of social improvement and projects of social inquiry. In fields of endeavour as diverse as agriculture, public health and meteorology the establishment of normal conditions provided a basis for scientific and social development. This period witnessed increasingly enthusiastic attempts to discover, through the collection and interrogation of statistics, the underlying causes and governing principles of a range of undesirable social phenomena: "suicide, crime, vagrancy, madness, prostitution, disease" (Hacking 1990: 3). Normality and deviance had become grist to the statistician's mill and, in the process, the question of evil a question of cause and effect.

The notion of normality can also be linked to another trend in

150

nineteenth-century European history, the rise of the nation-state and the increasing success of the political philosophy of nationalism. Anderson, B. (1983) and Gellner (1983) agree that the creation of a relatively homogeneous national culture is central to the modern nation-state. Both understand this national project, albeit in different ways, as a response to the requirements of industrial development, critically dependent upon a degree of mass literacy. Nurturing or imposing cultural conformity within state boundaries, nationalism took on board the "civilising process" which had been in train since the beginning of the early modern period (Elias 1978) and harnessed it to the demands of modernization and industrialization. This process required the elaboration of new social identities (with respect to nation, status and social class) and, in the field of morality, a considerable amount of internal missionary work by the churches and some pacification in the name of state law and order (for France, for example, see: Weber 1979: 241–77, 338–74).

However, nation building involved more than just identity and morality. There was also an instrumental concern with basic cultural competencies: language, literacy and numeracy. For the modern industrial state to succeed, its citizens had to be able to talk to each other, to read and to count. State education was central. The establishment in France of *les Ecoles Normales*, for example, tells us something, if only in respect to their name. Homogenization produced a hierarchy of cultural competencies which although distinct from the existing stratification of élite and popular culture, could not but be influenced by it. At the apex of the hierarchy, linguistic competence embodied, on the one hand, the national mother tongue which excludes minority ethnic cultures, and, on the other, the standardized language which excludes dialect.

Competencies in mathematics and related quantitative discourses had a different value and different implications for conceptions of normality. As nominally universal cognitive skills they offer less potential for nation building than language, literature or history. What they do promote – as indeed does the conflation of the ability to speak at all with the ability to speak in a particular way – is a notion of intellectual or cognitive normality embodied in the conception of IQ: measurable intelligence which has a statistically normal distribution in the population. From these roots diagnostic categories such as "mental subnormality", "educational subnormality", "mental retardation", "mental handicap", "special needs" and "learning difficulties" have been subsequently propagated.

There thus developed models of normal competence, its attributes and how they should be measured or graded. Incompetence became an identity – abnormality or subnormality – as did intellectual superiority. The one was to be controlled and discouraged (if necessary to the point of extermination), the other nurtured and supported. Both, of course, in the ultimate national interest. State-controlled education systems, with controlled curricula and staged formal testing and examinations, married the promotion of a minimal national cultural homogeneity to classifications of intellectual normality.

Combining a statistically-defined concept of normality with a model of national culture embodied in educationally-transmitted competencies produces a powerful arbitration of normality in the shape of assessment practices, of which there are a number of different versions (cf. Hanson 1993). In declining order of formality and scientific authority these include the diagnostic test, the written examination, the oral examination and the interview. The affinity between an ideologically-defined national cultural norm and a model of normal intellectual competence is clear, whether we consider the cultural bias of psychometric tests, the content of school curricula or the implicit assessment of criteria such as acceptability during oral examinations and interviews. Integrated by means of assessment practices into bureaucratic processes of administrative allocation (Batley 1981; Jenkins 1996), the concept of normality plays a strategic role in the patterned distribution of resources and penalties in modern societies.

There is, however, a further understanding of normality, also with nineteenth-century roots. By analogy with the organic contrast between health and morbidity, and drawing upon Comte, Durkheim, in *The rules of sociological method* (1964), distinguished the socially normal from the socially pathological thus: a social fact is normal when it is statistically typical for a particular kind of society (defined in evolutionary terms) and can be shown to be necessary to the stable functioning of that society (Durkheim 1964: 47–75). The pathological is dysfunctional or non-functional: a survival from an earlier phase, a symptom of the social state of anomie, or simply unusual or unnecessary. Durkheim's exegesis of sociological normality is followed by his celebrated analysis of crime as not only statistically normal, but also "an integral part of all healthy societies" (ibid: 67). As a model for understanding crime it entered the mainstream of Anglophone sociology through the mediation of Merton, and has since exerted an abiding influence on sociological criminology.

Durkheim's vision of normality has been so influential because it "uses a power as old as Aristotle to bridge the fact/value distinction, whispering in your ear that what is normal is also right" (Hacking 1990: 160). In the basic statistical model, normality is no more than the average. It can always potentially be improved upon and deviance in the top tail of the normal distribution may be desirable. Although Durkheim retains the idea that the normal is simply that which occurs most often, because he grounds this in a functionalist view of society which is modelled on an organic analogy, average normality becomes the criterion of social good health, any departure from which is pathological. Statistically-defined deviance becomes mapped onto culturally-defined deviance, in the identification of actual or potential social problems. This model of deviance and normality has an obvious elective affinity with the cultural project of nationalism, each reinforcing the other.

Four conceptual streams combine, therefore, in the late twentieth-century notion of normality. The *traditional* understanding, located within the specific and the particular, is that some things in the world are routine and to be expected. The *statistical* conception of normality as the most frequent or the average is embodied in a mathematically-defined curve of normal distribution which allows it both abstract expression and specific application. The notional *cultural* norm – subject and object of the nationalist project – has created "imagined communities" of inclusion and exclusion pre-dicated upon a degree of homogeneity. And finally, the view of normality as *health* derives from medical discourse and finds a sociological expression in Durkheim. The last three combine with the first in a pervasive and persuasive conflation of what is with what ought to be.

Deviance and power

Deviance does not just happen, and its constituent themes of social identity, morality and normality are not immaculate conceptions. We must look at actual social processes and the practices of actors within institutional and other contexts if we are to understand how deviance is socially constructed. Nor do I mean by that a mere putting into practice of notions about deviance. It is, rather, only in processes and practices that these notions are produced and reproduced at all. Drawing together the threads of the discussion so far, an outline emerges of four conceptually distinct processes connecting social identity, morality and normality in actors' lives.

Without proposing a hierarchy of importance, there is, first, the *classification of behaviour*. Culture signifies a repertoire of meaningful behaviour.[2] Within that realm of possibilities, discourses such as religion and law define, with greater or lesser clarity, degrees of moral acceptability, and, in the specification of appropriate sanctions, a tariff of severity with respect to deviance. They may also define the relationship between behaviour and group membership, classifying particular practices as more or less diagnostic of particular social identities. The law, as a literate discourse, is to some degree (although only to some degree) capable of establishing the cumulative consistency of statute and rule in its classifying practices. The same is true of bureaucratic regulation. However, much day-to-day moral classification of behaviour is neither regular, cumulative nor consistent. It is the improvisatory interpretive product of the constraints and possibilities of interaction. Behaviour can also be classified as normal or otherwise. Once again, while much of this classification is formally constituted – the product of authoritative diagnostic instruments and practices – much occurs within the ongoing social construction of routine in non-specialized social contexts.

Culture also maps out – formally and informally, explicitly and implicitly – a terrain of recognized social groups and categories, and the criteria for their membership, which is necessary for the classification of persons. These can range from citizenship and national identity to age grades. People may be included in, or excluded from, social identities by various combinations of emphasis of internal or external identification. Inclusion provides the context for appropriate individual moral evaluation, another dimension of the classification of persons (and exclusion may either be an exemption from moral judgement or the ultimate moral condemnation). The discourse of normality plays a particularly interesting role here in as much as, in addition to classifying individuals, it is explicitly constitutive of identity categories (and never more so than with respect to deviant abnormality). This may then feed back into the regulation and categorization of persons. Practices which classify behaviour and practices which classify people are likely to draw systematically and reciprocally upon each other.

Third, symbolization and ritual occur in many forms and in a range of institutional contexts: the religious, the legal, the medical and the political are simply the most obvious for the purposes of this discussion. Classificatory boundaries, whether of membership, morality or competence (and they can be intimately interwoven), may, for example, find expression in mythical discourse and the public celebration of history and tradition, they may be liturgically displayed in a dramatization of the penalties which attach to deviance and the rewards which accrue to conformity, or they may emerge objectively during the procedural set-pieces of employment selection. Processes and institutions of classification and social control themselves require legitimation, and ritual and symbolization are also important in this respect. While the symbolic power of ritual contributes to the authenticity of belief – and particularly in as much as this has affective foundations – in its dramatization of the consequences of deviance, for example, it may also be an element in the calculus of bad faith.

Finally, the importance of *social control and policing*, whether formal or informal, should not be forgotten. Despite the constraints provided by good and bad faith, some deviance is to be expected and some will be judged severe enough to require intervention. Following Durkheim, it is not altogether implausible to talk about deviance as necessary. Social control takes many guises: from gossip and ostracism, to being cared for, to expulsion and death. Each involves a stigmatization or transformation of the offender's identity, however minor, and a consequent reorientation of his or her place in society. In any situation, the relevance of a particular control strategy may be indicated or entailed by classificatory models of behaviour and of persons, its operation may be ritually elaborated and its results are likely to be of considerable symbolic moment. Social control practices mediate between the classification of behaviour and the classification of persons. The set pieces of social control, which are almost by definition wrapped in symbols and ritual, are likely to be simultaneously implicated in both modes of classification.

Symbol and ritual, in their turn, are bound up with the perpetual need to create and recreate the legitimacy of authority, suggesting that social control is only in part concerned with the specific persons who are its immediate objects as deviants. At least two other audiences are addressed. There is a general public *for* whom, rather than *of* whom, an example must be made, and whose support for the institutions and practices of social control is, even if only in an Althusserian final instance which never comes, conditional. Belief and bad faith are both at stake. In addition, however, agents of control themselves – be they Nuer leopardskin chief, Iranian revolutionary guard, British Lord Chief Justice or Louisiana lynch mob – will be more likely than not to create and experience their own practices as legitimate. The control of others is easier in the maximum possible good faith. To do so, justice must be justified and have its proper authority, and individuals agents must be properly authorized. Hence ritualization and symbolization. Deviance is thus only in part about deviants and may, in fact, be as much concerned with them as means than as ends.

Authority, legitimacy and control are words which serve to locate discourses of deviance within their proper social context: politics and power. Each of the processual strands which I have just outlined are organized within, structured by and contribute towards the operation of power relations. As a consequence, we have to ask who defines and manipulates the cultural codes which classify behaviour and persons, and in whose interests? What are the processes in and through which these codes are elaborated? Are certain categories of person more or less likely to be categorized as deviant? Similar questions must be posed with respect to ritual and symbolic discourses: Who is the custodian of orthodoxy? Who is symbolically powerful? How is such power acquired? What is the relationship between symbolic power and bureaucratic power? Last but not least, policing and social control are obviously deeply implicated in power relations: Who polices whom, and who polices those who police? Who determines the nature of social sanctions against deviance? And so on.

Foucault's well-known argument (1984) about the intimate relationship between power and knowledge – illustrated in this context by classificatory practices – has a bearing at this point. In its production and transmission, knowledge, for Foucault, is connected to power: truth and falsehood are defined politically. His argument that classification and categorization are central to the modern state's exercise of control over its citizens (1979) is equally familiar and germane. But perhaps most important of all is his insistence that one necessary product of the exercise of power is resistance. By this token, and bearing in mind the arguments of Becker and Douglas, not only are classificatory systems bound up with the exercise of power within societies and social groups, but they also necessarily create deviance: by definition and by way of resistance.

Clearly, not all deviance should be interpreted as resistance (or at least not without leeching the word of all of its historical resonances). But, to refer back to earlier elements in this discussion, it is possible to set Foucault's model alongside arguments such as Douglas's, that the intensity of group membership criteria and the visibility of the question of evil are related. Thus the legal elaboration and solidification of nationality and citizenship within the modern nation-state may contribute to a strengthening of categories of deviance. Parkin, drawing on Ricoeur, suggests (1985: 9–13) that, even before the development of modern state forms, the institutionalization of religion and social control in the emergence of ritual and legislative specialists lead to categories of moral classification becoming more definite and less contestable. Stanley Cohen, adopting an explicitly Foucauldian perspective, makes a cognate point. The classificatory work of assessment done by licensed, authoritative specialists such as psychologists and social workers is central to the modern social control project and tends to lead, despite the stated objectives of the professionals and the policies they pursue, to the raising and strengthening of boundaries of exclusion (Cohen, S. 1985).

None of which is to suggest that deviance is *only* a product of social control. The critique of the labelling perspective is too well-established and too well-rehearsed for such a proposition to be defensible (Gove 1980). Nor is the introduction of resistance as a factor in the social genesis of individuals who are identified, or who identify themselves, as deviant, sufficient acknowledgement of human agency in all of this. The discourses of identity, morality and normality are central to culture. They offer a repertoire for the understanding of others, in their identification and the attribution of motivation to them, and the possibility of a public discourse about deviance and deviants. Equally, however, they offer a repertoire for self-identification and the working up over time – over a lifetime, indeed, and whether in good faith or in bad faith – of internal discourses of motivation and justification. It is in the coming together of these two discourses, the external and the internal, that individuals become deviant.

Beyond deviance?

I have outlined a meta-disciplinary theoretical discourse about the social construction of deviance which synthesises arguments from sociology, social psychology and, particularly, social anthropology. It is sociologically axiomatic to say that deviance is relative. It is also, perhaps, trivial; to say this is not, in fact, to say very much. The central theme of my argument is that deviance is systematically relative, with respect to complex constituent discourses about social identity, morality and normality. It is possible to deviate or be classified as deviant with respect to each of these independently. Just as likely, allowing for the interpenetration of meaning in culture, is a synthesis of some or all of these elements, emphasized to different degrees, in any specific instance. Unpacking the notion of deviance in this fashion allows its theorization as a property of persons and behaviour in all local settings, and proper recognition of its historical and cultural variability. It is the job of research to delineate the pattern and shading, the weft and warp, of these strands in practice.

At this point, it may perhaps be appropriate to perform a minor about face, and to turn back briefly from anthropology to criminology. Why people commit crimes has always been one of the staple criminological questions. One of the standard critiques of the labelling perspective is that, in concentrating upon Lemert's secondary deviance – deviance which is the product of societal reaction and stigmatization – insufficient attention is paid to why people deviate in the first place (primary deviance). Looking at identity, morality and normality as distinct – even if inter-twined – modalities of deviance and crime introduces a varied landscape of possibilities with respect to *why* as well as *how* crime occurs, and it points us towards a more complex understanding of social reaction. Primary deviance is likely to differ widely and substantially in its aetiology, depending on the specific combination of these modalities in any given instance. The same can be said for the secondary deviance that emerges within the dialectics of reaction. Crime, in this understanding, becomes many things rather than one (not a strikingly original conclusion, but worth restatement).

Such an approach also suggests another conclusion. In important respects this chapter has not actually been about deviance at all (although it has, of course, been about deviance). Put in another way, this is the view – which is not in any sense original (Becker 1963: 3–8; Matza 1969: 41–66) – that it is only possible in the most superficial sense to construct a sociologically defensible category of deviance; that deviance and whatever is conventionally understood as its opposite are so much the same coin – not even different sides of it – that their divorce does a disservice to social analysis (J.R. Douglas 1970). The non-deviant – the mainstream, the good, the normal – should perhaps be our central focus of concern.

Although the paradox of sociologists who have advocated this "sceptical approach to deviance" (Cohen, S. 1971: 14) is that they have – doubtless for all sorts of good reasons – continued thereafter to research and write about deviance, this is an argument which requires restatement and, possibly, reinstatement. Problematizing the social construction of identity, morality and normality is central to a critical generic social science, and particularly to one which recognizes the theoretical centrality of culture. Accepting the arguments of this chapter, so too is the problematization of social categories of deviance. If so, it may be too important to remain ghettoized within a topical specialism called the sociology of deviance.

Notes

1 In March 1992, while I was visiting professor in the Institute of Ethnography and Social Anthropology at the University of Århus, Denmark, an invitation from the Centre for Cultural Studies, also at Århus, to deliver a public lecture, provided the stimulus to write the first version of this paper (published as *Arbejdspapir* no. 107 of the Centre). I am more grateful than I can say to my colleagues in Denmark for the warmth and enthusiasm then and subsequently, of their support and friendship. My final debt is to Simon Holdaway and Paul Rock for their enormously helpful and constructive critiques of an earlier draft.

2 *Meaningful* in this context does not imply that the behaviour should be necessarily meaningful to its author. For example, a physician may interpret an involuntary action of which the patient may not even be aware, or an observer attach a significance to the action of another which that other is neither aware of nor would understand (as in the social science case).

CHAPTER 9

Obituaries, opportunities and obsessions

Ken Pease

When I went to University College London in 1961 I was just turned 18 and cannot recall ever having met any real people who had been to university. Real people excluded teachers and the like. They had degrees, but their social distance only served to make me aware that a postman's son from a graduate-free extended family in Berkshire would be well out of his depth among students. And so he was. The degree was psychology, chosen without advice or much thought. Other students seemed so mature and urbane. How could I survive the exams at the end of the first year against such competition? It felt possible only by working harder than others did. I thus spent the first year not speaking in seminars, reading everything that was recommended and much that was not, which I did in the law library so as to avoid social contact with other psychology students which would reveal me as the fool I felt. In retrospect, that was an important year.

Two theoretical approaches first encountered then still influence me. The first (much favoured at the time) was the ethnological work of Lorenz (1970) (published in English) and Tinbergen (1953), among others. This was initially inductive, involving close observation over time for hypothesis development, which hypothesis was then tested experimentally. For example, the mating dance of the male three-spined stickleback was hypothesized to be a response not to the female as a whole, but to her swollen belly (the IRM or innate release mechanism in this case). This was tested experimentally, and it was confirmed that precise models which lacked a swollen belly did not trigger the dance, whereas crude models with a swollen belly did trigger it.

My father kept bees, and I had helped with them for much of my childhood, but von Frisch's work on bee communication (published in English 1967) staggered me with how much there was to see if you looked closely enough. This was to be reinforced years later by my PhD supervisor, a wise and eccentric psychiatrist who said that he learned more about physiology in disease from watching his sleeping patients than from the textbooks. Sticklebacks and bees don't talk (neither do sleeping patients). The impulse to look first at what goes in and what comes out and to ignore all the verbal gunk in between is particularly useful in criminology, where the elegance of that gunk (exemplified in judicial reasoning) is so high.

The second theoretical approach (not much favoured generally at the time, or indeed now) was George Kelly's personal construct theory, published in book form in 1955 (see also Bannister and Fransella 1971 for a more accessible and brief statement of personal construct theory and its implications). The theory's fundamental postulate, which I paraphrase, is that a person's processes are psychologically channelled by the ways in which he or she anticipates events. Thereby the distinctions a person makes between people, events and situations will restrict what is seen, encountered and decided.

How could anyone warm to two such different theories at the same time? Ethology mostly studied non-human animals (in fact the cynic's joke at the time was that an ethologist was an animal psychologist who actually liked animals). Kelly looked exclusively at people, and his data were their actions and their words. I have no satisfactory answer to the question, beyond the feeling that whatever Kelly found in people, in the last analysis it shaped their lives and behaviour, or it was epiphenomenal at best.

Days under the cupola at UCL library gave me two other enduring constructs. The first was that most famous psychologists were nice people who could make mistakes. The shaky evidence on which this (I think correct) conclusion was reached were the obituaries in the *Journal of Experimental Psychology* and the *American Journal of Criminology*. Being ever of a maudlin disposition (I dug graves in the vacations) I read every obituary in all the journal issues I ever opened. Clark L. Hull betting glasses of malted milk with his graduate students on the outcome of experiments filled me with delight. The snakes and ladders of careers in which minds were changed, hypotheses confirmed and friendships formed made the discipline human to me. The view of psychologists as warm and good people which the obituaries shaped in me has been largely confirmed by subsequent experience.

The final obsession which formed in my first year as a student was a delight in elegance and simplicity in research design and analysis. A personal hero was Stanley Schachter. The tenor of his work can best be described briefly by reference to one of his later studies. When researching the role of internal and external cues in determining reports of hunger in thin and obese people, he simply asked Jewish people how hungry they felt on fast days. Obese people felt less hungry than thin people while in the synagogue, but felt a lot hungrier while at home.

That kind of simplicity still gives me a frisson of pleasure, and is an attribute which is undervalued and (perhaps because of that) rare. I still think of criminology as a discipline whose contributing studies, with very few exceptions, lack elegance.

Graduate games

With hindsight, the two theoretical approaches described already underpin everything I have done professionally since. The ethologists began with close acquaintance with the specifics of their data. Kelly requires the consideration of how what is happening is constrained by the blinkers of the construct system. The two now feel inseparable. The virtues of the ethological approach are simply those of close observation and willingness to falsify hypotheses. The virtues of personal construct theory need further explication.

Personal construct theory was fully elaborated, and, uniquely among psychological theories of the time, was reflexive. That is to say, it could explain its own substance. Personal construct theory could be regarded as a set of constructs which could be considered in personal construct theory terms. This set it apart from popular theories of the time such as those of B.F. Skinner (see Skinner 1971 for the closest he came to a consideration of the issue). He took the view that humans, as other animals, should be regarded as empty organisms. The task of the psychologist was to uncover the rules which linked input and output. Yet one never got the sense that Skinner regarded his theories as the outcome of reinforcement contingencies like any other verbal product. Skinner spoke in London that year and I attended. Professor R.S. Peters asked Skinner a question about this. Skinner seemed not to see it as a problem.

Kelly had a set of 11 corollaries of his fundamental postulate. For example, sociality was dependent upon the ability to construe another person's constructions. Change was only possible when certain alternatives were sufficiently elaborated. This derives from Kelly's choice corollary which stated that a person chooses for herself that alternative in a construct whereby the greater elaboration of her system is possible. Less formally, you seldom choose to move from situations you understand (where your construct system is more elaborated) to those you understand less.

The values implicit in personal construct theory (at least as I read it) were that choice relies on the detailed specification of constructs, and that both education and clinical practice should be directed at understanding and detailing, and where necessary collaborating in the modification of, another person's construct system. In fact, Kelly was both educator and clinician, and he saw more similarities than differences in the two processes, both being concerned with the elaboration of unelaborated construct poles. For instance, in the construct Protestant/Catholic, bigotry is fuelled by an imbalance in the implications of each pole of the construct. Someone with an elaborated Protestant pole (i.e. who can explain the behaviours and beliefs of such a person) and an impoverished Catholic pole (i.e. where little is known about what it is to be Catholic) is liable to bigotry. The change process typically involves the elaboration of the implicit pole of the construct.

There are as many possible constructs as there are distinctions of which the imagination is capable, and each has a range of convenience. For instance, the sweet/sour construct has a range of convenience limited to foodstuffs and people. Take it much beyond that, and non-communication results. Habits of thought featuring numerous fragmented construct systems make theoretical thinking difficult. To anticipate, it is a feature of thinking about criminal justice that its components have distinct construct systems, each with a range of convenience limited to that component of the system. More than anything else, this is the feature of crime and justice which hampers a strategic approach.

Constructs are hierarchically organized, with a few core ones. These central constructs are most resistant to change. One crude way of getting to core constructs is the process of laddering. Starting with the peripheral construct of eating breakfast compared with not eating breakfast, a person is asked, "Is it better to have breakfast or not to have breakfast", to which she may answer, "Generally for me it's better to have breakfast". The next question is, "Why is it better to have breakfast?" The answer may be, "Because it stops you feeling hungry throughout the morning". The next question is, "Why is it better not to feel hungry throughout the morning?" and the answer, "Because it stops you working efficiently". The next question is, "Why is it better to work efficiently?" and the answer, "So that people can respect you and what you do". The next question is, "Why is it better for people to respect you and what you do?", and the next answer, "It just is". The point at which "It just is" comes up suggests a core construct. Starting from a range of "breakfast" type peripheral questions the sequence reveals a pattern of increasingly central constructs. Laddering can take place in the opposite direction (from core constructs outwards) by asking questions about what people are like who are respected. The answer will include a range of indicators, one of which may be the tendency to work efficiently. Personal construct theory thus comes with a toolbag of techniques to establish the shape and content of a person's construct system, and a tendency to think in terms of common and uncommon, adequate and inadequate construct systems for people in general. Moreover, it brings with it an inability to avoid thinking about the people with whom one interacts in personal construct terms. One of its particular virtues was what it was not. Although it could be regarded as a theory of psychotherapy (see Patterson 1973) it was not a grand theory whose implementation can degenerate into a sophisticated form of personal insult, as is Freudian theory. Neither is it a theory like Skinner's which makes a virtue of reducing the distinctively human. Skinner showed Skinner box traces from three species, and defied audiences to guess which trace was produced by which species. Although liable to criticism as overly

165

cerebral, in my view its potential has never been realized. As a social theory, it has the virtues of stressing the role and limitations of human agency, and of subsuming theories wherein human behaviour is conceived as driven by economic or social circumstance.

My first (and abortive) topic for doctoral research was about "sins of commission and omission".[1] It would be artificial to try and trace the influences of the two strands of thought described earlier as influential. The basic observation was that nearly all sets of moral rules were expressed as prohibitions. The Ten Commandments had nine prohibitions and one injunction, and I learned that the one injunction reflected a problem of translation. The Babylonian code of Hammurabi was the same, so were school rules, and so on. Why? Although abortive, the interest derived from noticing that a construct centring on, say, murder was better expressed as a prohibition than an injunction to behave in ways incompatible with murder. Clearly, personal construct elaboration would reveal why people are prohibited from action rather than enjoined to action by most moral codes. Not wishing to explore Hammurabi's personal construct system, I moved on. The piece of early research which best illustrates just looking at what people did and then working out the construct underpinnings concerns child pedestrian behaviour. It was carried out with Barbara Preston (Pease and Preston 1967). It came from going to schools with Barbara and just looking at what was done in the name of pedestrian education, and looking also at children crossing roads after school. At that stage, the form of words in use was the kerb drill. "Halt at the kerb. Eyes right, eyes left, eyes right again, and if all clear, quick march across the road." The name of drill, the use of militaristic language – halt, all clear, march – led young children to see the drill in a particular way. When they recited or acted out the drill, their shoulders were squared, heads thrown back and arms tight by their side, and swinging theatrically during the "march" across the road. This contrasted with the way they really crossed roads. In Kellian terms, the two kinds of behaviour had different ranges of convenience, with the kerb drill relevant in school (with a core construct of doing well, not doing well), and looking and running across having a range of convenience on real roads (with a core construct of being hurt/unhurt, perhaps). The disjunction was easy to show and is largely addressed in the Green Cross Code, which was developed in response to the research.

Personal constructs and criminal justice

Personal construct theory lends itself easily and interestingly to all aspects of criminology and penology. It can be considered both at the individual level, and in relation to commonalties among construct systems typical of a particular group or culture. The construct criminal/non-criminal seems to have a somewhat restricted range of convenience. Within that range (contacts between adult strangers or acquaintances) exploitative and violent behaviour will be construed as criminal. Outside that range, the same behaviour may be called discipline, bullying, reminding someone who's boss, going OTT, or foul or unsportsmanlike context, depending on whether the context is the school, the home, the workplace or the sports pitch. One of the ways of considering Norbert Elias's civilization hypothesis is that involves broadening the range of the criminal to include relationships with intimates, children and animals (see Garland, 1990).

Simply saying that construing an action as criminal has a limited range of convenience is too simple. At the criminal pole, victimizations per victim in early victimization surveys (before Sparks et al. 1976). Nobody knew that repeat victimization tends to be swift. The collection of data of this kind will lead to the development of constructs whose range of convenience extends from offender and judiciary. The notion of victim careers will be next for elaboration.

What are criminologists for?
a personal construct answer

There are two kinds of intellectual discipline. The first, "pure" science, seeks to identify the way the universe works, without reference to human exploitation of it. The second concerns the meshing of how nature works with human purpose. Such disciplines range from chemical engineering, through medicine and economics to social policy. The link between discipline types is more or less direct. In dentistry, the tooth is subject to basic physical and chemical processes. For dentistry, the contributing disciplines may make a direct contribution. However, for disciplines like economics, what is the equivalent of the tooth? Is it the economy; the currency; the consumer; the producer? Whatever it is, it is much more the product of human agency than the tooth. There thus exist a subset of applied disciplines where that which is to be explained is so completely a result of human social arrangements that pure disciplines are remote (though not irrelevant) to the determination of its processes. Criminology is such a discipline.

Intellectual enterprises like economics, social policy and criminology should seek to anchor themselves in the work of contributing disciplines. There is still a role for general theory. In criminology, this serves to locate and justify the fact that there are many more specific constructs concerning crime type and seriousness. There are behaviours in the school, in the home, on the sports field and workplace which are so serious that the criminal law would be invoked. The relationships between construct systems are subtle and various. Personal construct theory can cope with such subtlety. For example it distinguishes pre-emptive, constellatory and propositional constructs according to the relationships they have with other constructs.

At the level of the individual offender, we can consider the development of criminal identity in personal construct terms. At the point when the criminal pole is more elaborated than the non-criminal, a criminal identity is born. David Matza's (1969) techniques of neutralization have points of contact with personal construct theory, being the elaboration of the non-criminal pole so that there is no flip to criminal identity despite much offending. Interesting work on personal construct theory and criminal identity has been rare. Much interesting offender-based research suggests itself. What elaboration occurs for sex offenders and offenders against children and old people? In what way are the implications of that kind of behaviour elaborated, or (as Kelly might suggest) are they so completely unelaborated as to permit their contrast with other offenders? How are victims generally construed by their offenders?

Criminologists' constructs

Fundamental to the enterprise of criminology are the personal constructs of criminologists. For every distinction and research issue that could be identified in the criminological domain, there is more material about offenders than about any other group. Constructs surrounding motivation and childhood have a range of convenience limited to offenders, and those of selection, training and consistency were the issues whose range of convenience was restricted to the personnel of criminal justice. Try to research judicial motivation and you get short shrift (Knightley 1982). Research offender selection and (until recently) you would have been thought odd. In relation to the thinkable, in which all six topics have relevance to both offenders and practitioners of criminal justice, the collective construct system severely limited the research agenda.

The situation in criminology is only one version of the situation elsewhere. Social scientists ask one kind of question about those with power, and a quite different set of questions about those without it. Teachers and pupils, doctors and patients, managers and workers evoke different research questions. There is more research on the less powerful and the constructs in terms of which they are described and considered contrast markedly, with those in power being subject to broad appreciation, and those without to evaluation. In criminology, this contrast is one way of describing the origins of the "new criminology", where both punishing state and punished individual have roles to be considered according to same criteria. The new criminology could be described as an attempt to develop constructs with a range of convenience which could encompass all the actors in criminal justice.

Judges have almost always got off lightly at the hands of criminologists. In the best known characterization of sentencing, that between tariff and individualized measures, virtually any particular sentence can be justified by reference to the particular pole (tariff or individualized) of the core construct "correct sentencing". Little attention has been given to the specifics of sentencing (like the marked number preferences), or the heuristics which make them comprehensible (but see Fitzmaurice and Pease 1986). The fact that judges acknowledge influences verbally but appear unconstrained in practice has been demonstrated for rape (see Hebenton et al. 1994) and will no doubt be demonstrated wherever else a relevant study is mounted. The problem is one of making the study of judicial behaviour rather than judicial pronouncement the central subject of study. There is progress, and the very notion of criminal careers, into which newcomers are recruited, trained and from which they retire in due course indicates at least some progress in developing a more inclusive construct system for criminological research.

Criminal and victim

Most crime events require at least one victim and at least one offender. They can (in principle) be regarded as the two poles of the construct "crime participant". In Kellian terms, which is the more elaborated, i.e. what is known or believed about each of the participants? For criminology, until recently there was no question but that the criminal was more elaborated. In official statistics, that is still emphatically the case. You could regard the annual criminal statistics as the ossified version of the official construing of the crime event. That which is worth counting is counted and commented upon. That which is not worth counting is omitted. Note first that the annual statistical volume of central relevance is called *criminal* statistics. In its pages, you can gain huge amounts of information about defensible boundaries of criminal justice, and anomalies in the location of those boundaries. In social policy, consideration of the psychology of human need serves to locate the boundaries of social support, and anomalies in the location of these boundaries. Another way of saying this is that the theorist seeks to adjust the personal construct system of her readers. If a theory is radical enough, a paradigm shift is necessary. Another way of describing a paradigm shift is the substitution of one personal construct system for another. Conflict theory in criminology was an attempt to generate a paradigm shift.

Short of the grand theory, what can be the contribution of criminology? If grand criminological theory seeks to induce a paradigm shift, where should more modest criminological research be directed? In Kellian terms, a system is most resistant to change where the poles of the relevant construct are differentially elaborated. The example worked through above were the poles victim and perpetrator in the criminal transaction. There are many other examples in which one pole of a construct is dreadfully impoverished. Consider the construct drug use; the poles illegal and legal are wildly different in their degree of elaboration. Until the notion of what it would be like to live where drugs are legally available, the debate cannot happen. The implications of an inquisitorial legal system have not been elaborated, and a reasoned choice between that and an adversarial system cannot properly be made. More contentiously, I would argue that throughout criminal justice, the more punitive alternative is elaborated more fully than the less punitive alternative. Since punishment is mostly nasty, in this case the more elaborated pole is to be avoided.

However, the unelaborated pole can be nasty too. Considering an early stage in the criminal justice process, the decision may be made by the Crown Prosecution Service (CPS) to discontinue a case on the grounds of the insufficiency of evidence or of public interest. In making this decision, the focus (as is clear from the wording of guidance to prosecutors) is upon the adverse consequences of continuing. No attention is paid to the adverse consequences to the victim (and the police) of discontinuance. Furthermore, the CPS is in the bizarre (but not unusual) position in criminal justice of being protected from ever finding out the adverse consequences of the decision to discontinue. It is the *police* who have to tell the victim about discontinuance, not the CPS official. The CPS only get problems from the cases they allow to continue. Thus the decision to continue is negatively elaborated further and further, as is reflected in the ever increasing proportion of cases for discontinuance.

Casting around criminal justice for other contexts in which two poles of a construct have unequal elaboration, one needs go no further than the notion of miscarriages of justice. In principle, this phrase subsumes wrongful punishment and wrongful non-punishment. Yet in the literature and in the deliberations of the recent Royal Commission, wrongful punishment is virtually the sole subject of interest. In consequence, all the recommendations of the Commission are directed to the reduction of wrongful punishment. Whenever there is system pressure to reduce one kind of error, the other kind of error escalates (see Steadman and Cocozza 1974). The question arises – is it really the case that wrongful acquittal is trivial

171

in comparison with wrongful conviction? Was Sir William Blackstone really correct when he said that it is "better that ten guilty men escape than that one innocent suffers" (1809: 358)? Or is Blackstone and the practice of the justice system a victim of the consequences of the distorted development of the construct "miscarriage of justice"? There are legal reasons for which the wrongful acquittal remains so little elaborated. Its identification is the first hurdle, when there would be legal reluctance. However, it seems clear that wrongful acquittals outnumber wrongful convictions. In the particular case of rape, one author details cases in which people have been repeatedly acquitted of rape where charges were brought by different victims who did not know each other. It may be that, behind a Rawlesian veil of ignorance, we may wish the risks of wrongful acquittal and wrongful conviction to be more similar. They will not be so until the notion of wrongful acquittal is substantially elaborated.

The same asymmetry of implications is evident throughout the process, up to and including the decision to imprison. We all know the bad things about prison. Few know the bad things about the decision not to imprison, in terms of intimidation, further offending, police and community disenchantment, and so on.

The point is not whether one should favour punitive over other options. It is that the role of the criminologist should be largely to elaborate the impoverished poles of criminal justice constructs. To do this, the criminologist will probably be directed to the areas of least contention. It still entirely staggers me that victim concentration and its implications should have gone so unnoticed and unreflected in criminal justice information systems. Areas differ in their crime rates substantially because of the difference in the number of victimizations per victim (see Trickett et al. 1992) but this fundamental fact is neglected even in the most recent analysis of real crime rates (see Meithe and Meier 1994). It is amazing that debates about police accountability persist and there is little or no debate about the accountability of the Crown Prosecution Service despite the fact that by any defensible criterion the police are much more accountable.

Balancing the implications of constructs throughout criminal justice will not tell any policy-maker what to decide. Nor should it do so. Its role is to make it clear where there are decisions to be made, and make the decisions more informed – and probably more difficult.

Note

1 I cannot now trace the reference, but in the fake and funny journal for psychologists, *Worm Runners Digest*, the fate was described of a human who fell into alien hands. The aliens used Skinner boxes too, and the story is of the subject's attempts to behave in sufficiently bizarre ways to alert the alien psychologist to his intelligence. He succeeded only in getting the alien psychologist to label humanity as perverse and to recommend its destruction.

CHAPTER 10

Thinking about criminology: a reflection on theory within criminology

Simon Holdaway and Paul Rock

Ours is a culture of confession. Novels about incest, family conflict and sexual indiscretion are confessed as autobiography. Biographers have recently disregarded the wishes of their subject, revealing personal, tantalizing information more suited to the private than public sphere. Recently one of us watched a Channel 4 documentary in which a number of men confessed their use of prostitutes, apparently without concern for the effect on their partners, friends or family. One, who attributed the death of his wife to her discovery of his previously hidden behaviour, said tragically that he hoped that taking part in the programme would in part atone the wrong he had done. The men's individual lives and needs were paramount. It would not be surprising if a similar programme was found in next week's television schedules. The 1997 general election campaign was focused sharply upon the personal lives of parliamentary candidates and whether or not individuals could be trusted, including attempts to excavate any grubby details that provoked confession. In this book academic criminologists have written about the intertwining of personal lives and intellectual pursuits. Ours is a confessional culture.

This propensity to confess, in all its different forms, is not entirely new or disagreeable. The status of minorities, sexual minorities for example, can be changed when the apparently and abidingly normal "come out", challenging and normalizing deviance. Moral judgements and secure knowledge can be questioned radically when the previously secure appearance of the social world is fractured by confessional action. One result can be an enhancement of tolerance and understanding. Another is the promotion of gossip – imagine how impoverished we would be without it. A central claim of much social science is an ability to reveal, describe and analyse a terrain lying beneath the surface appearance of a society. Used with skill, from this perspective research findings can make a contribution to the creation of a more humane society.

A more negative aspect of a confessional culture is its signalling of the anonymity of modern societies. Persons are often only known in their individuality when brought to confession by the impersonal intrusion of a newspaper or television journalist. Hurt can be compounded in this setting, with a pressure to and an acceptance of a view that nothing short of "telling it like it is" is adequate, no matter the costs. Hypocrisy may be institutionalized when those whose trade is to write about the lives of others are less than reflexive about their own lives. In this volume Robert Reiner reminds us "woe to you scribes and Pharisees".

> I had always been mystified by the contrast between the theoretical Golden Rule ethic of Orthodox Judaism and the actual intolerance and lack of humane concern for others which is embodied in their moral and political conservatism. However, by the same token I have never been able to come to terms with the contrast between the egoism and inconsiderate treatment of people in personal relationships which is often accepted behaviour by those who nominally espouse values of radical concern for social justice. On a small-scale this disillusion set in at my very first staff meeting. Thirsting for some debate about intellectual or political matters, I was shocked to find the agenda dominated by heated discussions about car-parking spaces and the allocation of a merit increment (pp. 95).

Better, then, to reflect on how criminologists ply their trade than to ignore the taken-for-granted world of research and teaching as if it is unsullied by personal interest. What can be learned about the activity of theorizing within the context of individual lives from the various chapters of this book?

The personal and the theoretical

The notion of criminology as a science is etched clearly into its history. From this viewpoint, the criminologist does little more than facilitate a discovery of the social world. Personal values and beliefs are immaterial to the subjects researched and the findings of empirical work.

A cursory reading of many of the chapters in this volume, however, indicates that personal values and beliefs have an important role in the type of theorizing we reflect upon and mould within our research. Rather than distort excellent research, a commitment to a particular perspective, perhaps initially unrelated to academic work, can foster strongly theoretical and enlightened criminological writing. Betsy Stanko, for example, makes a clear link between her personal experience as a woman and the subsequent ways in which she has endeavoured to understand her research as an outworking of the "professional task",

> [which] as I see it, is to make visible that which is rendered invisible by organisational discourse, political rhetoric, and silence about inequity in the criminal justice systems which are rooted in unfairness within democratic states (Phillips 1993).

Clifford Shearing describes in graphic terms how the study of sociology enabled his reflection upon the system of apartheid in which he had grown up. Other contributors write about the social mobility that a university, social science education has opened up and their opportunity to consider the social world in a new way.

This encouragement to stand back and ponder the taken-for grantedness of the everyday world is sometimes borne from a reading of social science literature. Durkheim, Barth, Tilburg, Hutton and many other writers represent the diverse range of subject areas and perspectives of relevance to the ways in which our contributors have formed criminological research themes.

Understanding is sometimes borne from what Shearing called "poems", moments when we are surprised to find ourselves drawn to view phenomena in new ways, to theorize that which previously seemed unimportant, to think theoretically. In his chapter, Richard Jenkins makes the point that the creativity of interdisciplinary work, in his case between sociology and anthropology, can be enhanced by the development of a teaching programme.

Here we also encounter one of the contributions a university social science education can make to the formation of academic careers and, of more importance, the ideas graduates take into whatever sphere of work and relationships they pursue. There is now much pressure within universities to enhance an institutional research profile, which is in many ways the defining characteristic of the institution itself. The old universities, unlike schools, colleges of high education and, if truth be told, unlike some of the new universities, are surely distinct in that their staff research, publish and teach. Professors profess an intellectual subject and are expected to have published widely in that subject.

A danger facing us, however, is that for a number of reasons research could become virtually the sole priority. Having little face-to-face contact with their teachers, the next generation of social scientists, including criminologists, will have virtually no opportunity to ask them why they are persuaded by this and not that argument, to debate, and so on. The exciting and creative relationship between the activity of theorizing and the motivation of the researching, teaching criminologist will not be encountered. Theory will be diminished, relegated to something that is distant, written in books. If this trend continues we suspect that future generations of graduates who have encountered criminology in their studies will be less engaged by theory. Students will begin to think differently about criminology.

The context of research – for whom do I write?

The relative diminution of theory in criminology is surely related to changes in the funding base of research, especially the growth of policy-related research since the Brixton riots in 1981. After a rather heady period of radicalism during the 1970s, many criminologists realized that crime has a detrimental effect on the lives of the poor and that policy solutions are required. Policy related research then came to the fore, funded mostly by the Home Office and the ESRC.

An emphasis on theory does not require a neglect of policy. Theory can be enriched by a policy-related focus. However, the quest for research contract after research contract, with a related failure to find over-arching links that relate projects to each other theoretically: the growth of evaluation studies which neglect any intellectual base from which assumptions about the nature of social phenomena are developed; and the power funding bodies have established through a preoccupation with "users", by which they mean users whose voices claim legitimacy, has relegated writing about theory to a secondary position.

Criminologists increasingly write in the format of research reports, often for civil servants and other administrators. This is good and important. We are not arguing for the creation of a private world of criminological research. One consequence of this situation, however, is that many criminologists write for administrators and managers and forget that this is a particular readership with a very limited interest in the theoretical implications of findings. The whole gamut of performance indicators, added value, quality control and, importantly, the theoretical premises on which management is based frames too much research. Ken Pease reminds us that, from his theoretical perspective, the range of institutions of which particular research questions are asked has been constrained by unquestioned assumptions, posed by managers and at times by a co-opted criminology. Why, for example, is there so much attention given to the accountability of the police and very little to the Crown Prosecution Service? Why is it assumed that the public harm done by a failure to prosecute is less than that of an acquittal?

> Considering an early stage in the criminal justice process, the decision may be made by the Crown Prosecution Service to discontinue a case on the grounds of the insufficiency of evidence or of public interest. In making this decision, the focus (as is clear from the wording of guidance to prosecutors) is upon the adverse consequences of continuing. No attention is paid to the adverse consequences to the victim (and the police) of discontinuance. Furthermore, the CPS is in the bizarre (but not unusual) position in criminal justice of being protected from ever finding out the adverse consequences of the decision to discontinue (pp. 171).

New perspectives are sometimes realized when empirical

research listens to and articulates the voices of those who do not manage to. Nils Christie describes the way in which his work with people with learning difficulties has influenced his criminological thinking; how his search for the deviant monster has failed; and the ways in which this has touched upon his theoretical thinking. His chapter can be read as a rather utopian piece of writing, but its dismissal on the grounds of a lack of policy relevance would be perilous.

Among other important questions, Christie asks us to consider for whom we write? One of us has conducted Home Office funded research about the employment experience of black and Asian serving and erstwhile police officers (Holdaway and Barron 1997). During a difficult meeting with civil servants about the need to rewrite parts of a research report about resigners, to make it more "accessible", it became clear that this reasonable request meant that the voice of black and Asian resigners would be diminished. That was a seminal moment, awakening a realization that it was crucial in research not to neglect the voice of those evaluated and to reconsider questions about the ways in which the notion of race is socially constructed within particular institutions.

Standing at the boundary between a range of interests is the creative stance for a criminologist seeking to both inform policy discussion and to reflect upon the theoretical development of their ideas and subject area. Such a stance is very difficult because it means a capacity to engage with a wide range of interests seeking to pull research in different directions. We need to reflect carefully upon the implications of accepting the primacy of dominant voices, which not only silences the voices of those with less power and authority but also limits the theoretical richness of research.

The inevitability of theory

Criminology is a subject area, not a discipline and a disciplinary base for research is needed if any significant theoretical development is to be realized. Within this framework, criminology becomes what David Downes has called a rendezvous subject. Thinking theoretically within criminology therefore means being aware of the insights of one or more academic disciplines. A number of the criminologists writing in this volume mention the importance of their university education as an introduction to the theoretical base of their parent discipline. Ken Pease, for example, discusses psychological theories that have held his interest in many different subject areas; David Downes discovered sociological theory at the London School of Economics, and so on. Without wanting to give the ground to early development theorists, the theoretical puzzles which set the framework for undergraduate and, importantly, doctoral study, seem to have a lasting effect. But without a theoretical grounding in basic studies the subsequent work of many of our contributors and that of criminology more generally would have been impoverished.

Many, many more factors are also of importance in sustaining a theoretical framework for one's criminological research. Political commitments have been important to David Downes, Nils Christie and Betsy Stanko, for example. More personal experiences, Robert Reiner's childhood and youth within the context of orthodox Judaism, for example, have also played a part. Intellectual work embraces our lives in this sense.

Nothing here suggests that it is possible to reduce theory to autobiography. The excesses of standpoint theory in recent sociology (as if it was new) is a straitjacket that ignores the checks and balances found in theoretical thinking, the ways in which empirical data should influence analysis, and an awareness of the influence of academic writing on our own work. Both Frances Heidensohn and Betsy Stanko, working in different ways within a feminist frame-work, have chosen to mention the importance of intellectual ideas as well as their more practical, policy oriented concerns. Their research cannot be reduced to their engendered standpoint. It is nevertheless the case that a reflective criminology which seeks to enhance theory will be aware of the relationships between self and ideas, between the personal and the theoretical, but not be overly constrained by them.

This volume is therefore not a number of mere autobiographical accounts. As individual chapters, and as a whole, our contributors have written candidly about the various ways in which thinking about criminology develops theoretical and policy related ideas. Theory is inevitable and integral – without it criminology fades into an over-evaluated nothingness, speaking the language of managers, with intellectual horizons no more expansive than the next research contract.

By making accessible the ways in which a rather diverse group of criminologists have reflected upon their theoretical interests we hope to have emphasized the necessity, indeed the inevitability of theory within criminology. Part of our work as academic criminologists is to reflect similarly upon the influences playing on our research and writing. Clifford Shearing expresses this perspective of openness beautifully when he talks about what is perhaps the most important skill a social scientist can foster. Our subject matter is the flesh and blood, the relationships which entwine us all. To be reflective about the social world in all its ambiguity and complexity is to be open to new possibilities for criminological research. Would that we were more open to thinking about criminology creatively.

Like most people, I think, these "spirits" have emerged out of poetically charged experiences that have shaken me. Such moments are turning points, the figurative markers, in the narrative we construct as "our life". They are our poems, and it is these poems that lie at the root of our theories.

References

Adams, M. & R. Adams (eds) 1990. Introduction. *The problem of evil*. Oxford: Oxford University Press.

Adler, F. 1975. *Sisters in crime*. New York: McGraw-Hill.

Albemarle Report 1960. *The youth service in England and Wales*. London: Ministry of Education.

Anderson, B. 1983. *Imagined communities: reflections on the origins and spread of nationalism*. London: Verso.

Anderson, P. 1968. Components of the national culture *New left review* 50, July–August 1968 (Reprinted in P. Anderson 1992 *English Questions*. London: Verso Chapter 2.)

Aronson, E. (ed.) 1991. *The social animal*, 6th edn., New York: Freeman.

Austin, R. 1982. Womens liberation and increases in minor, major and occupational offences, *Criminology* **20**.

Bankowski, Z., G. Mungham, and P. Young, 1977. Radical criminology or radical criminologist? *Contemporary Crises* I, 45–6.

Bannister, D. & F. Fransella 1971. *Inquiring man*. Harmondsworth: Penguin.

Banton, M. 1964. *The policeman in the community*. London: Tavistock.

Banton M. 1965. *Roles*. London: Tavistock.

Barth, F. 1969. Introduction. *Ethnic groups and boundaries*, F. Barth (ed.). Oslo: Universitetsforlaget.

Batley, R. 1981. The politics of administrative allocation. *Urban political economy and social theory*, R. Forrest, J. Henderson & P. Williams (eds.). Aldershot: Gower.

Bayley, D. & H. Mendelsohn 1968. *Minorities and the police.* New York: Free Press.

Becher, T. 1989. *Academic tribes and territories.* Milton Keynes: Open University Press.

Becker, H.S. 1963. *Outsiders: studies in the sociology of deviance.* New York: Free Press.

Becker, H.S. (ed.) 1964. *The other side: perspectives on deviance.* New York: Free Press.

Bell, C. & H. Newby 1977. *Doing sociological research.* London: Allen and Unwin.

Ben-Yahuda, N. 1985. *Deviance and moral boundaries: witchcraft, the occult, science fiction, deviant sciences and scientists.* Chicago, Illinois: University of Chicago Press.

Berger, P.L. & T. Luckmann 1967. *The social construction of reality: a treatise in the sociology of knowledge.* London: Allen Lane.

Bertrand, M.A. 1992. Some concluding thoughts. See M.A. Bertrand, K. Daly, D. Klein.

Bertrand, M.A. 1994. 1893–1993: from La Donna Delinquent to a postmodern deconstruction of the "woman question" in social control theory. *Journal of Human Justice* 5(2), 43–57.

Bertrand, M.A., K. Daly & D. Klein (eds), 1992. *Proceedings of the international feminist conference on women, law and social control,* Mt. Gabriel, Quebec.

Bittner, E. 1974. Florence Nightingale in pursuit of Willie Sutton: a theory of the police. In *The potential for reform of criminal justice,* H. Jacob (ed.). Beverly Hills, California: Sage.

Blackstone, Sir W. 1809. *Commentaries V4.* 15th ed. London: Dawsons.

Blauner, R. 1964. *Alienation and freedom.* Chicago, Illinois: University of Chicago Press.

Bottoms, A. 1995. The philosophy and politics of punishment and sentencing. In *The Politics of sentencing reform,* C. Clarkson & R. Morgan. Oxford: Clarendon Press.

Bourdieu, P. 1990. *The logic of practice.* Cambridge: Polity.

Box, S. & C. Hale 1983. Liberation and female criminality in England and Wales. *British Journal of Criminology* 24(1).

Braithwaite, J. 1989. *Crime, shame and reintegration.* Cambridge: Cambridge University Press.

Brogden, M. & C. Shearing 1993. *Policing for a New South Africa.* London: Routledge.

Bryant, C.D. (ed.) 1990. *Deviant behavior: readings in the sociology of norm violations.* New York: Hemisphere.

Bumgartner, M.P. 1993. The myth of discretion. In *The uses of discretion,* K. Hawkins (ed.), 129–64. Oxford: Clarendon Press.

Bumiller, K. 1988. *The civil rights society.* Baltimore, Maryland: Johns Hopkins Press.

Cain, M. 1991. Paper delivered to International Feminist Conference on Women, Law and Social Control. Montreal.

Cain, M. 1973. *Society and the policeman's role.* London: Routledge.

Cain, M. 1990. Realist philosophy and standpoint epistemologies, or feminist criminology as a successor science. See Gelsthorpe & Morris (1990), 124–40.

Campbell, B. 1993. *Goliath: Britain's dangerous places.* London: Methuen.

Carlen, P. 1984. Justice: too important to be left to the judiciary? *The Abolitionist* **16**(4), 8–10.

Carlen, P. 1985. *Criminal women.* Oxford: Polity Press.

Carlen, P. 1992. Criminal women and criminal justice: the limits to, and potential of, feminist and left realist perspectives. In *Issues in realist criminology*, R. Matthews & J. Young (eds), 51–69. London: Sage.

Carlen, P. & A. Worrall (eds) 1987. *Gender, crime and justice.* Milton Keynes: Open University Press.

Cavadino, M. & J. Dignan 1992. *The penal system.* London: Sage.

Chatterton, M. 1995. The cultural craft of policing – its past and future relevance. *Policing and Society* **5**:2.

Christie, N. 1952. Fangevoktere i konsentrasjonsleire/*Guards in concentration camps*/*Nordisk Tidsskrift for Kriminalvidenskab*s. 439–458 **40**, og **41** 44–60.

Christie, N. 1960. *Tvangsarbeid og alkoholbruk.* /*Forced labour and use of alcohol*/Oslo: Universitetsforlaget.

Christie, N. 1996a. Sosial kontroll./*Social control*/87–95. In C. Høigård og L. Finstad (ed.). *Kriminologi.* Oslo: Pax.

Christie, N. 1996. Kriminologi./*Criminology*/In E. Boe (ed.) *Veien mot retsstudiet* 340–47. Oslo: Tano-Aschehoug.

Christie, N. 1971. *Hvis skolen ikke fantes. En studie i skolens sosiologi* /*If the school did not exist*/Oslo: Universitetsforlaget 157 s. German edition: *Wenn es die Schule nicht gäbe. Ketzerisches zur Schulreform*, München 1974. Paul List.

Christie, N. 1972. *Fangevoktere i konsentrasjonsleire/Guards in concentration camps*/Oslo: Pax.

Christie, N. 1973. *Hvor tett et samfunn?/How tightly knit a society?*/Oslo/ Copenhagen, new and enlarged edition 1982. Oslo: Universitetsforlaget Copenhagen Ejlers forlag.

Christie, N. 1981. *Limits to pain.* Oxford: Robertson.

Christie, N. 1989. *Beyond loneliness and institutions. Communes for extraordinary people.* Oslo: Norwegian University Press.

Christie, N. 1993. *Crime control as industry: towards GULAGS, western style?* London: Routledge.

Christie, N. & K. Bruun 1985. *Den gode fiende. Narkotikapolitikk i Norden/ The useful enemy. Drug-policy in the Nordic countries.* Oslo/ Copenhagen: Universitetsforlaget, Ejlers. New and enlarged edition 1995. Also in German; *Der nützige Feind. Die Drogenpolitik und ihre Nutzniesser.* 1991 Bielenfeld AIZ.

Cloward, R. 1963. *Social problem: social definitions and social opportunities.* New York: unpublished.

Cohen, A.P. 1985. *The symbolic construction of community.* London: Tavistock/Ellis Horwood.

Cohen, L. & M. Felson 1979. Social change and crime rate trends: a routine activity approach. *American Sociological Review* **44**, 588–608.

Cohen, S. 1971. Introduction. In S. Cohen (ed.) *Images of deviance.* Harmondsworth: Pelican.

Cohen, S. 1972. *Moral panics and folk devils.* London: MacGibbon and Kee.

Cohen, S. 1981. Footprints in the sand: a further report on criminology and the sociology of deviance in Britain. In M. Fitzgerald, G. McLennan & J. Pawson (eds), *Crime and society.* Routledge: London.

Cohen, S. 1985. *Visions of social control.* Cambridge: Polity.

Cohen, S. 1988. *Against Criminology.* New Brunswick, New Jersey: Transaction.

Cohn, E.G. & D.P. Farrington 1994. Who are the most influential criminologists in the English-speaking world? *British Journal of Criminology* **34**(2), 204–25.

Collins, P.H. 1991. *Black feminist thought.* London: Routledge.

Connell, R. 1987. *Gender and power.* Stanford, California: Stanford University Press.

Cooney, M. 1994. Evidence as partisanship. *Law and Society Review* **28**, 833–58.

Crane, D. 1972. *Invisible colleges: Diffusion of knowledge in scientific communities.* Chicago, Illinois: University of Chicago Press.

Crank, J. 1994. Watchman and community: myth and institution-alization in policing. *Law & Society Review* **28**, 325–51.

Crawford, A., T. Jones, T. Woodhouse & J. Young 1990. *The second Islington crime survey.* London: Middlesex Centre for Criminology.

Crenshaw, K. 1994. Mapping the margins: intersectionality, identity politics, and violence against women of color. In *The public nature of private violence*, M.A. Fineman & R. Mykitiuk (eds), 93–118. London: Routledge.

Crowther Report 1959. *15 to 18* London: Ministry of Education.

Dahrendorf, R. 1987. The underclass and the future of Great Britain. Lecture delivered at Windsor Castle, 27 April.

Daly, K. 1989. Criminal justice ideologies and practices in different voices: some feminist questions about justice. *International Journal of the Sociology of Law* **17**, 1–18.

Daly, K. 1994. *Gender, crime and punishment*. New Haven, Connecticut: Yale University Press.

Daly, K. & M. Chesney-Lind 1988. Feminism and criminology. *Justice Quarterly* **5**, 497–538.

Davis, M. 1990. *City of quartz: excavating the future in Los Angeles*. London: Verso.

Deakin, N. 1995. Regenerating cities: mans and ends. In *Social Policy and the City*, H. Jones & J. Lansley (eds). Aldershot: Avebury.

Deutscher, I. 1968. *The non-jewish Jew and other essays*. Oxford: Oxford University Press.

Dewey, J. 1929. *Experience and nature*. New York: W.W. Norton.

Digest 2 1993. *Information on the criminal justice system in England and Wales*. London: Home Office.

Dixon, B. & E. Stanko 1993. *Serving the people: sector policing and local accountability*. Report to Islington Police and Community Safety Unit. Centre for Criminal Justice Research, Brunel University.

Dixon, B. & E. Stanko 1995. Sector policing and public accountability. *Policing and Society* **5**(3), 171–83.

Dixon, D. 1996. Change in policing and changing police. In *The Australian and New Zealand Journal of Criminology*, **28** (Special Supplementary issue) 62–6.

Docklands Forum 1990. *Employment in Docklands*. London: Birkbeck College.

Douglas, J.R. (ed.) 1970. *Deviance and respectability: the social construction of moral meanings*. New York: Basic Books.

Douglas, M. 1966. *Purity and danger: an analysis of concepts of pollution and taboo*. London: Routledge and Kegan Paul.

Douglas, M. 1973. *Natural symbols: explorations in cosmology*. Harmondsworth: Pelican.

Downes, D. 1966. *The delinquent solution*. London: Routledge.

Downes, D. 1976. *Gambling, work and leisure*. London: Routledge & Kegan Paul.

Downes, D. 1988. *Contrasts in tolerance*. Oxford: Oxford University Press.

Downes, D. & F. Flower 1965. *Educating for uncertainty*. London: Fabian Society.

Downes, D. & R. Morgan 1994. Hostages to fortune? The politics of law and order in post-war Britain. In *The Oxford handbook of criminology*, K. Maguire, R. Morgan & R. Reiner (eds). Oxford: Clarendon.

Downes, D. & P. Rock (eds) 1979. *Deviant interpretation*. Oxford: Martin Robertson.

Downes, D. & P. Rock 1988. *Understanding deviance: a guide to the sociology of crime and rule breaking*. 2nd edn. 1995. Oxford: Clarendon Press.

Durkheim, E. 1964. *The rules of sociological method*. New York: Free Press.

Elias, N. 1978. *The civilising process*. Oxford: Basil Blackwell.

Elkins, D. 1995. *Beyond sovereignty*, Toronto: University of Toronto Press.

Emerson, R. & B. Paley 1993. Organizational horizons and complaint-filing. In *The uses of discretion*, K. Hawkins (ed.) 231–48. Oxford: Clarendon Press.

Fielding, N.G. 1991. Conflict and change in Britain Series – *The police and social conflict: rhetoric and reality*. London: Athlone Press.

Fitzmaurice, C. & K. Pease 1986. *The psychology of judicial sentencing*. Manchester: Manchester University Press.

Forrester, D., K. Pease, M.R. Chatterton 1988. *The Kirkholt burglary prevention project, Rochdale*. London: Home Office.

Foster, J. 1990. *Villains*. London: Routledge.

Foucault, M. 1977. *Discipline and punish*. London: Allen Lane.

Foucault, M. 1979. *Discipline and punish: the birth of the prison*. Harmondsworth: Peregrine.

Foucault, M. 1984. Truth and power. In *The Foucault reader*, P. Rabinow (ed.). Harmondsworth: Peregrine.

Foucault, M. 1988. On problematization. *History of the present*. Spring, 16–17.

Freilich, M., D. Raybeck, J. Savishinsky (eds) 1991. *Deviance: anthropological perspectives*. New York: Bergin and Garvey.

Friedan, B. 1963. *The feminine mystique*. New York: Dell.

Friel, B. 1981. *Translations*. London: Faber and Faber.

Fyvel, T. 1961. *The insecure offenders*. London: Chatto and Windus.

Gabor, D. 1963. *Inventing the future*. London: Secker and Warburg.

Galbraith, J. 1959. *Affluent society*. London: Hamish Hamilton.

Gamble, A. 1988. *The free economy and the strong state*. London: Macmillan.

Gardner, C. B. 1995. *Passing by: gender and public harassment*. Berkeley, California: University of California Press.

Garfinkel, H. 1967. *Studies in ethnomethodology*. Englewood Cliffs, New Jersey: Prentice-Hall.

Garland, D. 1990. *Punishment and modern society*. Oxford: Clarendon.

Garland, D. 1997. Governmentality and the problem of crime, forthcoming in *Theoretical Criminology*.

Gellner, E. 1983. *Nations and nationalism*. Oxford: Basil Blackwell.

Gelsthorpe, L. 1992. Response to Martyn Hammersley's paper "On feminist methodology". *Sociology* **26**(2), 213–18.

Gelsthorpe, L. & A. Morris 1988. Feminism and criminology in Britain. *British Journal of Criminology* **28**, 223–40.

Gelsthorpe, L. & A. Morris 1990. *Feminist perspectives in criminology.* Buckingham: Open University Press.

Gilligan, C. 1982. *In a different voice.* Cambridge, Massachusetts: Harvard University Press.

Goffman, E. 1963. *Stigma: notes on the management of spoiled identity.* Englewood Cliffs, New Jersey: Prentice-Hall.

Goldthorpe, J., D. Lockwood, F. Bechhofer, J. Platt 1968. *The affluent worker: political attitudes and behaviour.* Cambridge: Cambridge University Press.

Goldthorpe, J., D. Lockwood, F. Bechhofer, J. Platt 1969. *The affluent worker in the class structure.* Cambridge: Cambridge University Press.

Gordon, C. 1991. Governmental rationality: an introduction. In *The Foucault effect: studies in governmentality*, G. Burchell, C. Gordon & P. Miller (eds). Hempel Hempstead: Harvester Wheatsheaf.

Gordon, M. & S. Riger 1988.*The female fear.* New York: Free Press.

Gould, S. 1996. Full house. New York: Harmony Books.

Gould, S. 1997. An orderly way of life, in *Independent on Sunday*, January 5.

Gove, W.R. (ed.) 1980. *The labelling of deviance: evaluating a perspective.* Beverley Hills, California: Sage.

Griffith, J.A. 1977. *The politics of the judiciary.* London: Fontana.

Hacking, I. 1990. *The taming of chance.* Cambridge: Cambridge University Press.

Hagan, J., J. Simpson & A. Gillis 1979. The sexual gratification of social control. *British Journal of Sociology* **30**(1), 25–38.

Hall, S. et al. 1978. *Policing the crisis: mugging, the state and law and order.* London: Macmillan.

Hammersley, M. 1992. On feminist methodology. *Sociology* **26**(2), 187–206.

Hanmer, J., J. Radford & E. Stanko (eds) 1989. *Women, violence and policing.* London: Routledge.

Hanson, F.A. 1993. *Testing testing: social consequences of the examined life.* Berkeley, California: University of California Press.

Harding, S. (ed.) 1987. *Feminism and methodology.* Milton Keynes: Open University Press.

Harvey, D. 1989. *The condition of postmodernity.* Oxford: Blackwell.

Heady, P., S. Smith, V. Avery. 1994. 1991 Census validation survey. London: HMSO.

Hebenton, W., R. Ranyard & K. Pease 1994. An analysis of a guideline case as applied to the offence of rape. *Howard Journal* **33**, 203–17.

Hegel, F. 1836. *Philosophy of right*. London: George Bell and Sons.

Heidensohn, F. 1968. The deviance of women: a critique and an enquiry. *British Journal of Sociology* **19**, 160–75.

Heidensohn, F. 1969. Prison for women. *Howard Journal*.

Heidensohn, F. 1985. *Women and crime*. London: Macmillan.

Heidensohn, F. 1991a. Introduction: convergence, diversity and change. In *Crime in Europe*, F. Heidensohn & M. Farrell (eds). London: Routledge.

Heidensohn, F. 1992. *Women in control? the role of women in law enforcement*. Oxford: Oxford University Press.

Heidensohn, F. 1994. Gender and crime. In *The Oxford handbook of criminology*, M. Maguire, R. Morgan & R. Reiner (eds) 997–1039. Oxford: Oxford University Press.

Heidensohn, F.M. 1970. Sex, crime and society. In *Biosocial aspects of sex*, G.A. Harrison (ed.). Oxford: Blackwell.

Heidensohn, F.M. 1986. Models of justice: Portia or Persephone? some thoughts on equality, fairness and gender in the field of criminal justice. *International Journal of The Sociology of the Law* **14**.

Heidensohn, F.M. 1989. *Crime and society*. London: Macmillan.

Heidensohn, F.M. 1994b. We can handle it out here. Women officers in Britain and the USA and the policing of public order. *Policing and Society* **4**(4).

Heidensohn, F.M. 1995. Taking charge: crime and social control in the twentieth century. Inaugural lecture Goldsmiths College.

Heidensohn, F.M. 1997. Crime in policing. In *The future of Europe*, V. Symes, C. Levy, J. Littlewoods (eds). London: Macmillan.

Heidensohn, F.M. & M. Farrell (eds) 1991. *Crime in Europe*. London: Routledge.

Heidensohn, F. & M. Silvestri 1997. The conformity of criminology. In *Merging themes in British criminology*, J. Vaag & T. Newburn (eds). Loughborough: British Society of Criminology.

Hester, S. & P. Eglin 1992. *A sociology of crime*. London: Routledge.

Higher Education Report. 1963. London: HMSO. Cmnd 2154.

Hobbs, D. 1988. *Doing the Business*. Oxford: Clarendon Press.

Hobbs, D. 1996. *Bad Business*. Oxford: Oxford University Press.

Hobsbawm, E. 1994. *Age of extremes: the short twentieth century 1914–1991*. London: Michael Joseph.

Holdaway, S. 1979. *The British police*. London: Arnold.

Holdaway, S. 1983. *Inside the British police*. Oxford: Blackwell.

Holdaway, S. 1991. *Recruiting a multi-racial police force*. London: HMSO.

Holdaway, S. 1995. Culture, race and policy: some themes in the sociology of the police. *Policing and Society* **5**:2.

Holdaway, S. 1996. *The racialisation of British policing*. Basingstoke: Macmillan.

Holdaway, S. & A.-M. Barron 1997. *Resigners? the experience of Black and Asian police officers*. Basingstoke: Macmillan.

Holmwood, J. 1995. Feminism and epistemology: what kind of successor science? *Sociology* **29**(3), 411–28.

Holy, L. & M. Stuchlik 1983. *Actions, norms and representations: foundations of anthropological inquiry*. Cambridge: Cambridge University Press.

Hughes, E.C. 1961. Good people and dirty work. *Social Problems* **10**:1.

Hutton, W. 1995. *The state we're in*. London: Jonathan Cape.

James, O. 1995. *Juvenile violence in a winner–loser culture*. London: Free Association Books.

Jencks, C. & R. Peterson (eds) 1991. *The urban underclass*. Washington, DC: Brookings.

Jenkins, R. 1977. Witches and fairies: supernatural aggression and deviance among the Irish peasantry. *Ulster Folklife* **23**, 33–56.

Jenkins, R. 1982. *Hightown rules: growing up in a Belfast housing estate*. Leicester: National Youth Bureau.

Jenkins, R. 1983. *Lads, citizens and ordinary kids: working-class youth life-styles in Belfast*. London: Routledge and Kegan Paul.

Jenkins, R. 1992. *Pierre Bourdieu*. London: Routledge.

Jenkins, R. 1994. Rethinking ethnicity: identity, categorisation and power. *Ethnic and Racial Studies* **17**, 197–223.

Jenkins, R. 1996. *Social identity*. London: Routledge.

Jenkins, R. 1997. *Rethinking ethnicity: arguments and explorations*. London: Sage.

Jones, S., 1986. *Policewomen and equality*. London: Macmillan.

Jones, T., T. Newburn, D. Smith 1994. *Democracy and policing*. London: Policy Studies Institute.

Judge, T. 1968. *The first fifty years*. London: The Police Federation.

Judge, T. 1994. *The force of persuasion*. London: The Police Federation.

Kaufmann, W. 1963. *The faith of a heretic*. New York: Anchor.

Kelly, G. 1995. *The Psychology of Personal Constructs*. 2 vols.

Kelly, L. 1988. *Surviving sexual violence*. Oxford: Polity.

Kinsey, R., J. Lea, J. Young 1986. *Losing the fight against crime*. London: Blackwell.

Klein, D. 1973. The aetiology of female crime: a review of the literature. *Issues in Criminology* **8**(2), 3–30.

Klockars, C. 1980. The dirty Harry problem. *The Annals* **452**: November.

Knightley, P. 1982. Judges block Whitelaw on sentencing in courts. *Sunday Times*, 24 Jan.

Kuhn, T. 1970. *The structure of scientific revolutions.* Chicago, Illinois: University of Chicago Press.

Lafferty, T. 1932. Some metaphysical implications of the pragmatic theory of knowledge. *The Journal of Philosophy.* 14 April. **XXIX.** 206.

Lambert, J. 1970. *Crime, police and race relations.* Oxford: Oxford University Press.

Lea, J. and J. Young 1984. *What is to be done about law and order.* Harmondsworth: Penguin.

Lemert, E. 1972. *Human deviance, social problems and social control,* 2nd edn. Englewood Cliffs, New Jersey: Prentice Hall.

Levi, M. 1993. The extent of cross border crime in Europe. *European Journal of Criminal Policy and Research* **1**(3).

Levi, M. 1995. Correspondence in *British Journal of Criminology* **35**, 1.

Livingstone, S. 1996. On the continuing problem of media effects. In *Mass media and society,* J. Curran & M. Gurevitch (eds). London: Arnold.

Lockwood, D. 1958. *The black-coated worker.* London: Allen and Unwin.

Lorenz, K. 1970. *Studies in animal and human behaviour.* 2 vols., London: Methuen.

MacInnes, C. 1959. *Absolute beginners.* London: MacGibbon & Kee.

MacInnes, C. 1961. *England, half English.* London: MacGibbon & Kee.

MacIntyre, A. 1981. *After virtue.* London: Duckworth.

MacKinnon, C.A. 1979. *The sexual harassment of working women.* New Haven, Connecticut: Yale University Press.

MacKinnon, C.A. 1982. Feminism, marxism, method, and the state: toward feminist jurisprudence. *Signs* **4**, 635–58.

MacKinnon, C.A. 1987. *Feminism unmodified.* Cambridge, Massachusetts: Harvard University Press.

MacKinnon, C.A. 1990. *Toward a feminist theory of the state.* Cambridge, Massachusetts: Harvard University Press.

Macnicol, J. 1987. In pursuit of the underclass. *Journal of Social Policy.*

Maguire, M., R. Morgan & R. Reiner (eds) 1994. *The Oxford handbook of criminology.* Oxford: Oxford University Press.

Manning, P. 1993. The preventive conceit. *American Behavioral Scientist* **36**, 639–50.

Manning, P. 1977. *Police work.* Cambridge, Massachusetts: MIT Press.

Marenin, O. 1983. Parking tickets and class repression: the concept of policing in critical theories of criminal justice. *Contemporary Crises* **6**:2.

Marquand, D. 1988. *The unprincipled society.* London: Cape.

Martin, J.P. & G. Wilson 1969. *The police: a study in manpower.* London: Heinemann.

Martin, S.E. 1979. POLICEwomen and police women: occupational role dilemmas and choices of female offenders, *Journal of Police Science and Administration* **2**(3), 314–23.

Matza, D. 1969. *Becoming deviant*. Englewood Cliffs, NJ: Prentice-Hall.

Mays, J. 1964. *Crime and the social structure*. London: Faber.

McLennan, G. 1995. Feminism, epistemology and postmodernism: reflections on current ambivalence. *Sociology* **29**(3), 391–410.

Meithe, T.D. & R.F. Meier 1994. Crime and its social context. Beverley Hills: Sage.

Melossi, D. 1994. The "economy" of illegalities: normal crimes, elites and social control in comparative analysis. In *The futures of criminology*, D. Nelken (ed.), 202–19. London: Sage.

Messerschmidt, J. 1993. *Masculinities and crime*. Lanham, Maryland: Rowman & Littlefield.

Messerschmidt, J.W. 1995. From patriarchy to gender: feminist theory, criminology and challenge of diversity. See N. Rafter & F.M. Heinensohn (eds).

Milgram, S. 1965. Some conditions of obedience and disobedience to authority. *Human Relations* 57–75.

Millett, K. 1970. *Sexual politics*. London: Virago.

Mills, C. 1959. *The sociological imagination*. New York: Oxford University Press.

Mitchell, J. 1971. Women's estate. Harmondsworth: Penguin.

Morgan, R. & R. Reiner (eds) 1994. *The Oxford handbook of criminology*. Oxford: Oxford University Press.

Morgan, R., R. Reiner & I. McKenzie 1990. *Police powers and policy: a study of custody officers*. Final report to the Economic and Social Council.

Morris, A. 1987. *Women, crime and criminal justice*. Oxford: Blackwell.

Muir, Jr., K.W. 1977. *The police: streetcorner politicians*. Chicago, Illinois: Chicago University Press.

Murray, C. 1994. *Underclass: the crisis deepens*. London: Institute for Economic Affairs.

Murray, C. & R. Herrnstein 1994. *The bell curve: intelligence and class structure in American life*. New York: Free Press.

National Association for the Care and Resettlement of Offencers (NACRO) 1995. *Crime and social policy*, appendix 3. London: NACRO.

Naffine, N. 1987. *Female crime*. Sydney: Allen and Unwin.

Nelken, D. (ed.) 1994. *The futures of criminology* . London: Sage.

Newburn, T. & E. Stanko (eds) 1994. *Just boys doing business?* London: Routledge.

Nietzsche, F. 1989. *On the genealogy of morals and ecce homo*. In W. Kaufmann (ed.). New York: Vintage.

Oakley, A. 1972. *Sex, gender and society*. London: Temple Smith.

Osborne, D. & T. Gaebler. 1993. *Reinventing government*. New York: Plume.

Pain, R. 1993. *Crime, social control and spatial constraint: A study of women's fear of crime*, Unpublished PhD thesis, University of Edinburgh.

Parkin, D. 1985. Introduction. In *The anthropology of evil*, D. Parkin (ed.). Oxford: Basil Blackwell.

Patterson, C.H. 1973. *Theories of counselling and psychotherapy*. New York: Harper and Row.

Pearce, F. 1976. *Crimes of the powerful*. London: Pluto Press, and Box, S. 1983. *Power, Crime and Mystification*, London: Tavistock.

Pearson, G. 1983. *Hooligan: a history of respectable fears*. London:

Pease, K. & B. Preston 1967. Road safety education for young children. *British Journal of Educational Psychology* **37**, 305–313.

Peirce, C. 1934. *Collected papers*. Cambridge, Massachusetts: Harvard University Press. V. 314.

Peirce, C. 1934. *Collected papers*. Cambridge, Massachusetts: Harvard University Press.

Phillips, A. 1993. *Democracy and difference*. Cambridge: Polity.

Phillipson, M. 1970. *Thinking out of deviance*. Unpublished paper.

Pitch, T. 1990. *Limited Responsibilities: social movements and criminal justice*. London: Routledge.

Pitch, T. 1995. Feminist politics, crime, law and order in Italy. In *Engendering criminology: the transformation of a social science*, N. Rafter & F.M. Heidensohn (eds). Buckingham: Open University Press.

Pocock, D. 1985. Unruly evil. In *The anthropology of evil*, D. Parkin (ed.). Oxford: Basil Blackwell.

Practical ways to crack crime. London: Home Office Publications Office.

Punch, M. & T. Naylor 1973. The police – a social service. *New Society*. 17 May.

Quinney, R. 1970.*The social reality of crime*. Boston, Massachusetts: Little, Brown.

Radford, J. 1987. Policing male violence – policing women. In *Women, violence and social control*, J. Hanmer & M. Maynard (eds), 30–45. London: Macmillan.

Radford, J. 1989. Women and policing: Contradictions old and new. In *Women, policing and male violence*, J. Hanmer, J. Radford & E. Stanko (eds), 13–45. London: Routledge.

Rafter, N. 1985. *Partial justice: women in state prisons 1800–1935*. Boston, Massachusetts: Northeastern University Press.

Rafter, N. & F. Heidensohn 1995. Introduction: the development of feminist perspectives in criminology. In *Engendering criminology: the transformation of a social science*, N. Rafter & F. Heidensohn (eds). Buckingham: Open University Press.

Rafter, N.H. & E.A. Stanko (eds) 1982. *Judge, lawyer, victim, thief: women, gender roles and criminal justice*. Boston, Massachusetts: Northeastern University Press.

Ramazanoglu, C. 1989. Improving on sociology: problems in taking a feminist standpoint. *Sociology* 23(3), 427–42.

Ramazanoglu, C. 1992. On feminist methodology: male reason versus female empowerment. *Sociology* 26(2), 207–212.

Rawlings, P. 1995. The idea of policing. *Policing and Society* 5, 129–49.

Reiner, R. 1976. Reds in blue? *New Society* 7 October.

Reiner, R. 1978a. *The blue-coated worker*. Cambridge: Cambridge University Press.

Reiner, R. 1980. Forces of disorder. *New Society* 10 April.

Reiner, R. 1991. *Chief constables*. Oxford: Oxford University Press.

Reiner, R. 1992a. *The politics of the police*, 2nd edn. Hemel Hempstead: Wheatsheaf.

Reiner, R. 1992b. Policing a postmodern society. *Modern Law Review* 55:6.

Reiner, R. 1992c. Police research in the United Kingdom: a critical review. In *Modern policing*, N. Morris & M. Tonry (eds). Chicago, Illinois: Chicago University Press.

Reiner, R. 1993. Race, crime and justice: models of interpretation. In *Minority ethnic groups and the criminal justice system*, L. Gelsthorpe & B. McWilliam (eds). Cambridge: Institute of Criminology.

Reiner, R. 1994a. The mystery of the missing crimes. *Policing Today* 1(2), 16 December.

Reiner, R. 1995b. The dialectics of Dixon: changing television images of the police. In *Police force, police service: care and control*, M. Stephens & S. Becker (eds). London: Macmillan.

Reiner, R. 1996a. The case of the missing crimes. In *Interpreting official statistics*, R. Levitas & W. Guy (eds). London: Routledge.

Reiner, R. 1996b. Crime and control: an honest citizen's guide. *Sociology Review* April.

Reiner, R. 1996c. Crime and the media. In *LSE on social science: a centenary anthology*, H. Sasson & D. Diamond (eds). London: LSE Publishing.

Reiner, R. 1996d. *Policing*. Aldershot: Dartmouth.

Reiner, R. & M. Cross (eds) 1991. *Beyond law and order*. London: Macmillan.

Reiner, R. & S. Spencer (eds) 1993. *Accountable policing: effectiveness, empowerment and equity*. London: Institute for Public Policy Research.

Reiss, Jr. A.J. 1968. Stuff and nonsense about social surveys and observation. In *Institutions and the person*, H. Becker et al (eds). Chicago, Illinois: Aldine.

Reiss, Jr. A.J. 1971. *The police and the public.* New Haven, Connecticut: Yale University Press.

Reynolds, G.W. & A. Judge 1968. *The night the police went on strike.* London: Weidenfeld and Nicholson.

Robinson, C. 1978. The deradicalisation of the policeman. *Crime and Delinquency* 24:2.

Rock, P. 1973a. *Making people pay.* London: Routledge and Kegan Paul.

Rock, P. 1973b. Phenomenalism and essentialism in the sociology of deviance. *Sociology* 7(7), 17–29.

Rock, P. 1974. Conceptions of moral order. *British Journal of Criminology* 14(2), 139–49.

Rock, P. 1979. *The making of symbolic interactionism.* London: Routledge and Kegal Paul.

Rock, P. 1986. *A view from the shadows: the ministry of the solicitor general of Canada and the making of the justice of victims of crime initiative.* Oxford: Clarendon Press.

Rock, P. 1988. The present state of criminology in Britain. *British Journal of Criminology* 28, 58–69.

Rock, P. 1990. *Helping victims of crime.* Chapter VII. Oxford: Clarendon Press.

Rock, P. 1991. *Helping victims of crime: the home office and the rise of victim support in England and Wales.* Oxford: Clarendon Press.

Rock, P. 1994. The social organisation of British criminology. See Maguire et al. (1994).

Rock, P. 1995. The opening stages of criminal justice policy making. *British Journal of Criminology* 353, 1–16.

Rose, D. 1996. *In the name of the law: the collapse of criminal Justice* London: Jonathan Cape.

Rose, N. & P. Miller 1992. Political power beyond the state: problematics of government. *British Journal of Sociology* 43(2), June.

Rowntree Foundation 1995. *Inquiry into income and wealth.* York: Joseph Rowntree.

Russell, D.E.H. 1982. *Rape in marriage.* New York: Free Press.

Rutter, M. & H. Giller 1983. *Juvenile delinquency: trends and perspectives.* Harmondsworth: Penguin.

Schutz, A. 1967. Common-sense and scientific interpretation of human action. *Collected Papers* 1. The Hague: Martinus Nijhoff.

Shapland, J. et al. 1995. Milton Keynes, *Criminal justice audit: institute for the study of the legal profession.* Sheffield: Faculty of Law, University of Sheffield.

Shearing, C.D. 1984. *Dial-a-cop: a study of police mobilisation*. Toronto: Centre of Criminology, University of Toronto.

Shearing, C.D. & Stenning, P.C. 1983. Private security: implications for social control. *Social Problems* **30**(5), 493–506.

Simon, J. 1995. Rights of humanity, rites of sovereignty: punishment, immigration, and the phantom of the nation state. Paper presented at the Centre of Criminology, University of Toronto, Toronto, Canada, 19 October.

Simon, R.J. 1975. *Women and crime*. London: Routledge.

Simpson, S. 1989. Feminist theory, crime and justice. *Criminology* **27**, 605–31.

Simpson, S. & L. Elis 1995. Doing gender: Sorting out the caste and crime conundrum. *Criminology* **33**, 47–81.

Skinner, B.F. 1971. Beyond freedom and dignity. Harmondsworth: Penguin.

Skolnick, J. 1966. *Justice without trial*. New York: John Wiley.

Smart, C. 1976. *Women, crime and criminology: a feminist critique*. London: Routledge and Kegan Paul.

Smart, C. 1977. *Women, crime and criminology*. London: Routledge and Kegan Paul.

Smart, C. 1979. The new female criminal: reality or myth. *British Journal of Criminology* **19**(1).

Smart, C. 1989. *Feminism and the power of law*. London: Routledge and Kegan Paul.

Smart, C. 1990. Feminist approaches to criminology or postmodern women meets atavistic man. In *Feminist perspectives in Criminology*, L. Gelsthorpe & A. Morris (eds). Buckingham: Open University Press.

Smith, D. 1983. *Police and people in London*. London: Policy Studies Institute.

Smith, D. 1990. *Texts, facts and femininity*. London: Routledge.

Smith, M.G. 1960. *Government in Zazzau 1800–1950*. London: Oxford University Press for the International African Institute.

South, N. 1996. Late-modern criminology: "Late" as in "Dead" or "Modern" as in "New"? In *After sociology? contemporary reflections on the state of the discipline*, D. Owen (ed.). London: Sage.

Sparks, R. 1992.*Television and the drama of crime*. Buckingham: Open University Press.

Sparks, R., H. Genn, D. Dodd 1977. *Surveying victims*. London: Wiley.

Stanko, E. 1977. *These are the cases that try themselves*. Unpublished PhD thesis, City University of New York.

Stanko, E. 1981–2. The impact of victim assessment on prosecutors' screening decisions: the case of the New York County district attorney's office. *Law & Society Review* **16**, 225–240.

Stanko, E. 1981. The arrest versus the case. *Urban Life* **9**, 395–414.

Stanko, E. 1982. Would you believe this woman? In *Judge, lawyer, victim, thief*, N. Rafter & E. Stanko (eds), 63–82. Boston, Massachusetts: Northeastern University Press.

Stanko, E. 1983. Hidden fears. *The Guardian*.

Stanko, E. 1985. *Intimate intrusions: women's experience of male violence*. London: Routledge.

Stanko, E. 1987. Hidden violence against women. In *Victims: a new deal?*, M. Maguire & J. Pointing (eds), 40–46. Milton Keynes: Open University Press.

Stanko, E. 1988. Fear of crime and the myth of the safe home: a feminist critique of criminology. In *Feminist perspectives on wife abuse*, M. Bograd & K. Yllo (eds), 75–88. London: Sage.

Stanko, E. 1989. Missing the mark: policing battering. In *Women, policing and male violence*, J. Hanmer, J. Radford & E. Stanko (eds), 46–69. London: Routledge.

Stanko, E. 1990a. *Everyday violence: how women and men experience physical and sexual danger*. London: Pandora.

Stanko, E. 1990b. When precaution is normal: A feminist critique of crime prevention. In *Feminist perspectives in criminology*, L. Gelsthorpe & A. Morris (eds), 173–83. Milton Keynes: Open University Press.

Stanko, E. 1991. *Policing local violence*. Report to the Home Office, Crime Prevention Unit, London.

Stanko, E. 1993a. Feminist criminology: an oxymoron? Paper presented to British Criminology Conference, Cardiff, Wales.

Stanko, E. 1995b. Policing domestic violence: dilemmas and contradictions. *Australian and New Zealand Journal of Criminology*, special supplement, 31–44.

Stanko, E. 1996a. Reading danger: sexual harrassment, anticipation and self-protection. In *Women, violence and male power: feminist research, activism and practice*, M. Hester, L. Kelly & J. Radford (eds), 50–62. Buckingham: Open University Press.

Stanko, E. 1996b. Warnings to women: police advice and women's safety in Britain. *Violence Against Women* **2**, in press.

Stanko, E. & K. Hobdell 1993. Assault on men. *British Journal of Criminology* **33**(3), 400–415.

Stanley, L. (ed.) 1990. *Feminist praxis*. London: Routledge.

Steadman, H.J. & J.J. Cocozza 1974. *Careers of the criminally insane: excessive social control of deviance*. Lexington: DC Heath.

Sumner, C. 1994. *The sociology of deviance: an obituary*. Buckingham: Open University Press.

Tajfel, H. 1981. Social stereotypes and social groups. In *Intergroup behaviour*, J.C. Turner & H. Giles (eds). Oxford: Blackwell.

Taylor, I., P. Walton & J. Young 1973. *The new criminology*. London: Routledge and Kegan Paul.

Thompson, E. P. 1980. *Writing by candlelight*. London: Merlin.

Thompson, E.P. 1975. *Whigs and hunters: the origin of the black act*. London: Allen Lane.

Tinbergen, N. 1953. *The social behaviour of animals*. London: Methuen.

Titmuss, R. 1960. *The irresponsible society*. London: Fabian Society.

Trickett, A., D.K. Osborn, J. Seymour, K. Pease. 1992. What is different about high crime areas? *British Journal of Criminology* **32**, 81–90.

Tuan, Y. 1979. *Landscapes of fear*. Oxford: Basil Blackwell.

Turner, B. 1990. *...and the policeman smiled: 10,000 children escape from Nazi Europe*. London: Bloomsbury.

Turner, V.W. 1974. *The ritual process: structure and anti-structure*. Harmondsworth: Pelican.

Van Maanen, J. 1973. Observations on the making of policemen. *Human Organisation* **32**(4), 407–18.

Von Frisch, K. 1967. *The dance, language and orientation of bees*. Oxford: Oxford University Press.

Waddington P. 1986. Mugging as a moral panic. *British Journal of Sociology* **37**.

Walklate, S. 1989. *Victimology*. London: Unwin Harman.

Watson, J.D. 1968. *The double helix*. New York: Atheneum.

Weber, E. 1979. *Peasants into Frenchmen: the modernization of rural France 1870–1914*. London: Chatto and Windus.

Weber, M. 1964. *The theory of social and economic organization*. Talcott Parsons (ed.). New York: Free Press.

Weber, M. 1978. *Economy and society: an outline of interpretive sociology*, G. Roth & C. Wittich (eds). Berkeley, California: University of California Press.

Weber, M. 1918. Politics as a vocation. In *From Max Weber*, H. Gerth & C.W. Mills (eds). London: Routledge.

White, J. 1985. *When words lose their meaning*. Chicago, Illinois: University of Chicago Press.

Whyte, W. 1951. Observational field-work methods. In *Research methods in social relations*, M. Jahoda (ed.) 510–11. New York: Dryden Press.

Wiles, P. & A. Bottoms 1995. Crime and insecurity in the city, Paper delivered to Mannheim Centre, London.

Wilkins, L. 1964. *Social deviance*. London: Tavistock.

Williams, P. 1991. *The alchemy of race and rights*. Cambridge, Massachusetts: Harvard University Press.

Wilson, J.Q. 1968. *Varieties of police behaviour*. Cambridge: Harvard University Press.

Wootton, B. 1959. *Social science and social pathology.* London: Allen & Unwin.

Wright, E.O. 1976. Class boundaries in advanced capitalist societies. *New Left Review* **98**, July/August, 3–42.

Young, M. 1958. *The rise of the meritocracy.* London: Thames and Hudson.

Young, A. 1990. *Femininity in dissent.* London: Routledge.

Young, J. 1994. Incessant chatter: recent paradigms in criminology. See Maguire et al. (eds) (1994).

Young, M. 1991. *An inside job.* Oxford: Clarendon Press.

Young, V. 1992. Fear of victimization and victimization rates among women: a paradox? *Justice Quarterly* **9**, 421–41.

Index